Build a Yurt

"The surface of the earth is soft and impressible by the feet of men; and so with the paths which the mind travels. How worn and dusty, then, must be the highways of the world, how deep the ruts of tradition and conformity."
Henry David Thoreau, Walden

LEN CHARNEY

Build a Yurt

The Low-Cost Mongolian Round House

Illustrations by
Margie Smigel and
Barbara Anger

Collier Books
A Division of Macmillan Publishing Co., Inc.
New York

Collier Macmillan Publishers
London

In memory of my father, my finest teacher, who combined lessons in diligence, craftsmanship, and understanding to lay the foundation for my own progress.

Macmillan Publishing Co., Inc.
866 Third Avenue, New York, N.Y. 10022
Collier-Macmillan Canada Ltd.

Library of Congress Cataloging in Publication Data

Charney, Leonard.
  Build a yurt.

  1. Yurts. I. Title.
[TH4870.C47   1974b]   690'.8   74-513
ISBN 0-02-079320-0

First Collier Books Edition 1974

Build a Yurt is also published in a hardcover edition by Macmillan Publishing Co., Inc.

Design by Bob Antler

PRINTED IN THE UNITED STATES OF AMERICA

Acknowledgments

There are many people who provided me with much needed assistance in completing this book, and I would like to extend many thanks for their efforts.

My appreciation to Margie Smigel and Barbara Anger who worked on such short notice to turn out such fine illustrations; to Ken Davis for many long hours of service in the darkroom slaving over dense, underexposed negatives; to Mike Stahl for photo guidance, development and design; to Chuck and Laurel Cox for clarifying facts about yurts in America; to Schuyler Cammann of the University of Pennsylvania for information and encouragement; to Rich Tannen for past assistance in yurt construction and design as well as numerous discussions regarding this book's format; to the students of Cape Elizabeth High School, Cape Elizabeth, Maine and friend Chris Cox for his assistance; to the administration and faculty of Antioch Graduate School in Harrisville, New Hampshire, especially the late Dr. Norm Wilson; to my sister, Anita, for her persistent encouragement and professional assistance; to my mother for aid, consideration and rearing me on great chicken soup; to Omar and Betty Mulks for their boundless generosity in making the yurt experience so worthwhile; and finally to Shelley Stahl, whose love, kindness, valuable criticism, organizational common sense and unending patience enabled me to make this book a reality.

Contents

Introduction

In the spring of 1970 I was still an undergraduate and had been exposed to near-ly every living arrangement there is available to the college student. I had sur-vived a 9-by-12 university dorm cubicle, complete with a roommate of someone else's choosing, uncontrollable and unbearable steam radiators, sterile white paper-thin walls, and noisy, inconsiderate beer drinking, poker playing neighbors. The following year I moved into a fraternity house, also a loud, expensive, and disconcerting environment. From here it was out to the "country," four miles from campus to a new, poorly constructed, modern duplex, split level, overlooking the valley, next to the pig farm, "country house." Whatever motivated me to wish that upon myself I'll never know, but unfortunately I did sign the lease and live in it for four months. It was perhaps after moving out and finding a tiny single room in a boardinghouse near campus that I began to recognize the nature of my discontent. I sat down one evening in late winter and computed that in two and a half years I had spent almost $1,500 to live in places that did barely more than provide minimal shelter. I had been completely at the mercy of people and institutions simply because they owned land on which sat ugly buildings which were able to house the lowly student. And because of this advantage they were able to subject me to uncomfortable quarters and charge outrageous rent. My present room was a bit more tolerable, since the cost was more reasonable, yet it was incredibly confining and did not afford me the degree of privacy in the appealing surroundings that I desired. It was time for something to be done but at first it appeared that I had exhausted the options open to me. The next few days a friend, who lived in a slum downtown, and I discussed the alternatives we might investigate. We agreed that each of us wanted a place that would be inexpensive, private, and removed from the clutches of the greedy landlord. Our first idea was to renovate a barn. Both of us were familiar with the use of tools and had acquired a moderate amount of carpentry skills. It was probably at this point that it began to impress me how important it was to be able to design and construct one's home and build into the shell a proper living environment. Thereupon we set out to find a farmer who had an old barn that was in disuse and at the same time was not beyond repair. After two weeks of crisscrossing and circumventing the countryside, putting up with the grunts and guffaws of so many farmers, we finally found the place we had been looking for. This particular fellow who owned the barn seemed eager for such a venture to be made and we gradually came to realize that his major concern was to be able to charge exorbitant rents for that ideal place in the country after we'd moved on. But for us it was to be strictly Easy Street—he would not charge rent while we lived there. Fortunately for us, we never began the project. Once we checked out the expense involved for building permits, restoring timbers, insulation, heat, plumbing, wiring, and insurance, it turned out that each of us would be spending as much as, if not more than, we had in two and a half years.

Our next brainstorm was to check out the cost of building our own place from scratch. Initially, we investigated the prospects of building an A-frame, but estimates convinced me that it cost too much, and visiting some of the A-frames that had been built in the area for summer homes showed me that they wasted too much space to make them worth the investment. Next came the traditional log cabin, but in order to build it ourselves, we would have to cut the logs, which for the non-landowner are not readily available, and allow them to season properly. This perhaps would have been a splendid idea if we had had the time to wait for the wood to be readied. An old fellow about twenty-five miles out of town ran a small sawmill operation and cut out prefab log cabins for the folks in the area. Many a hunter had one nestled somewhere up in the woods for use as a lodge during the fall and winter seasons. All of them were tight, well-fitting dwellings, with two opposite slabs of each log sheared off a few inches to create a snug, flush surface. In all his cabins, chinking was therefore unnecessary. The least expensive model, a 20 × 20-foot unpartitioned larch structure, cost $800 and at first glance appeared suitable for our needs. Upon further consideration we realized that we had not taken into account the costs of partitioning, which would very definitely be required if we were to succeed in attaining the kind of privacy we had in mind. Dividers would also cut into the utilitarian nature of the cabin.

Another possibility that we considered briefly was the geodesic dome, yet I found the structure forbidding and unappealing. I must admit that I have never spent much time in a dome, but there has always been something plastic and almost hostile about the design.

Needless to say, our attempts to find adequate alternatives in housing were not moving right along. It appeared that we'd have to settle for a ramshackle slab cabin, using planks and plywood. Such was the state of things when I heard about a nearby commune and how the people on it were living in yurts. Several young people had joined together a couple of years prior to my search and bought one hundred acres of land in a nearby community. The only dwelling for human inhabitance at the time they made their purchase was a fine old log cabin. This served well as a communal kitchen and meeting place, yet each member wanted his or her own structure for sanity and solitude. The yurt, which had already been introduced to the area a few years back, was perfect to suit their needs. These circular latticework dwellings averaged 16 feet in diameter and utilized ordinary building supplies for construction. It was a structure that was inexpensive to build, requiring relatively little expertise to erect. In this communal environment, the yurt could be put together in a short period of time, since the people worked collectively whenever extra hands were required. Here was an attractive, organic dwelling that blended in with any rustic setting. I was amazed on entering a yurt for the first time to find a building that looked quite tiny from the outside, yet provided spacious accommodations for a couple of people. At the same time, it was perhaps one of the most congenial atmospheres I had ever encountered. Indeed there are few people who can step inside the yurt and not be moved by its coziness and almost immediate sense of security. As you can imagine, I was no exception. Once I had observed a few of the yurts and seen how each individual had

INTRODUCTION

ix

utilized the basic structure in various fashions to suit personal desires, it became quite obvious that I was going to have to find a place to build and call a yurt my home.

My friend opted for the slab cabin, yet when he would come to visit in the depth of winter, walking the few hundred paces from his electrically lit, bottled gas-heated cabin, he would always stay a while, talking by the shadows of the kerosene lamp and taking great pleasure in stoking the wood fire, his eyes wandering throughout the yurt up to the starlit skylight. When I would leave my home for extended periods of time, he would inevitably move from his cabin to stay in my yurt.

This book, then, is more than a simple set of instructions and a practical guide to building a yurt, though for certain I have attempted to include them in great detail. One does not simply tell how to build a yurt without sharing part of the experience of living in one, as well as telling some of the interesting things and about some of the people encountered along the way. In fact, it is impossible to speak about yurts without recalling such things as personal satisfaction and triumph, coupled with the instances when I observed and was part of that almost forgotten art of being neighborly.

The stories of living in a yurt are endless. It is a true tale of completion, wonder, and ritual. It is the essence of a worthwhile education—one that I now invite you to begin.

Build a Yurt

Before we take a more careful look at the yurt as it has evolved in America and talk about its construction, it is perhaps important to pause briefly and consider the yurt with regard to its Mongolian heritage. By doing so, you will be more apt to appreciate its design as you actually build and inhabit one. Answers to questions you will be confronted with as you work alone, as well as those that are asked by folks who assist you in your endeavor, will come quite naturally. Thus the entire venture will be that much more valuable for everyone involved. Personally, I regret that I did not know very much about the Mongolian yurt as I was building mine and assisting in the assembly of so many others, for I realize that there are things that I would have done differently out of deference to its inventors. In addition, the beauty of its simplicity and ingenious design would have been that much more apparent. As I have discovered these things through research and in the course of correspondence, and in turn have spoken to other yurt dwellers who were also unaware of such things as traditions and religious significance behind the yurt, I sensed that these people as well were imbued with new impressions about their own homes. To build your own shelter is an overwhelmingly valuable and important thing to do, but I now realize that in the case of such a

The Mongolian Yurt

structure as the yurt, which is so alien to Western architecture, it is of equal import not to be insensitive to the heritage of the design and the people who are responsible for its origin.

The Mongolian Ger

If one were to inquire of a Mongolian about the state of his yurt, he might simply stare at you in bewilderment, or perhaps ask you to excuse yourself for making strange noises in his presence. And if he were truly incensed, he might even ask that you leave his home. For the Mongolian, the proper term is *ger*, meaning "dwelling," and yurt or yurta is the Westerner's term as it was so labeled by Russian merchants, traders, and marauders of many years ago.

Accounts of nomadic herdsmen inhabiting these collapsible felt tents date back as far as the time of Marco Polo. When Genghis Khan was busy piecing together his Mongolian empire in the thirteenth century, the ger was providing shelter for the wandering Mongolian, his family, and his animals.

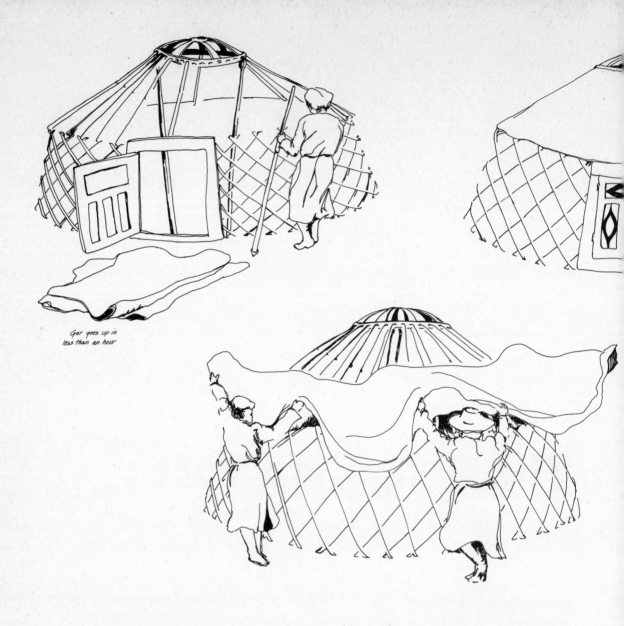

Ger goes up in
less than an hour

Why a Yurt?

Looking at the yurt's structure one begins to see why it was such an appropriate form of housing for these people. The Mongol required a home that was very portable. When the grazing became inadequate, he needed to be able to pack his belongings quickly and move on to a place where his animals could have a better chance of surviving. The traditional yurt was perfect, for it could be erected in half an hour and disassembled in about as much time. The entire yurt, consisting of all the wood pieces, canvas, and felt could be loaded on the back of a camel, or other animal of burden, and transported to the next destination.

The climate was another factor that had to be taken into consideration when selecting the proper shelter. It called for a structure that would be easy to heat and have a great capacity for thermal retention in the bleak winters, also standing up against winds that would at times approach ninety miles an

hour. In the summer when the sun would beat down and scorch the unprotected earth, this same dwelling would have to be able to breathe and offer protection for its inhabitants. Once again the yurt was ideal in meeting these demanding requirements. The streamlined shelter was such that high winds would not threaten to blow the building over, as is sometimes the danger with its square or rectangular rivals. Rather they would slip around the curved walls, leaving the yurt and its residents unaffected. The circular, uncluttered design would prevent the warm air from getting lost in tiny corners while its flow would not be impeded by obstructive beams or supports. The small fire in the center hearth would be more than adequate, even with the small hole at the top of the conical roof open to allow the passage of the smoke and cooking fumes. I recall one account I read of a cold winter night in the Mongol's tent that demonstrated the ease with which those inside were kept warm. As the sun fell, so did the outside temperature. Members of the household entered the yurt, also letting in their baby yaks, calves, and lambs, as well as a pregnant sheep. In this particular instance the place became so warm that the family had to sleep nearly naked, shedding their warm fur coverings. Even when the winds would howl and the temperature would drop to fifty or sixty below zero, the family would be quite comfortable sleeping on piles of rugs, wrapping themselves with furs and quilts.

When summertime rolled around, the yurt was adaptable enough that it could easily conform to the changes in the natural environment. What was done quite simply was that several of the outer layers of felt were removed to create a more permeable surface. The part of the canvas and felt closest to the ground was rolled up, leaving the latticework walls exposed, also making for more substantial ventilation. One other alteration for their warm season was the excavation of a trench ringing the yurt to prevent the home from becoming inundated with water during periods of heavy rainfall.

Another feature of the yurt that seemed to lend itself beautifully to the nomad's existence was the relative ease with which the yurt could be cleaned. Certainly this was a consideration, once you stop to imagine the condition of the yurt after so many humans and various animals mingled in the same space over a period of time. The way in which the yurt was dusted and tidied is probably a novel one as seen through the eyes of the Westerner. The procedure was concise and efficient. The family would peel the felt covering from the wooden framework and move all of the yurt's furnishings to the outside. Everyone would take up a position somewhere around the wall and carry the yurt skeleton bodily fifty or so feet windward. From here it was a question of placing all the quilts and boxes in their designated positions inside and once again attaching the felt and canvas skin. I laughed when I read this description in an old *National Geographic* and thought how much sense it made. If only life could be so uncluttered and precise in America's humble homes.

Here's another thought that I throw out about the practical nature of the yurt. Because of the flexible latticework skeleton and the tremendous degree of weight and tension distribution, the yurt dweller need never worry about the consequences of an earthquake. Now this might not be of any real significance to someone living in a non-earthquake region, but it might be a comforting fact for anyone living along the San Andreas Fault!

The Skeletal Structure of the Mongolian Ger

Although most of the yurts that have been built in the United States are of a permanent design, the emphasis on the Mongolian models for the rural areas was to construct something very portable. The ger was therefore made from a series of components that were assembled on a particular site. Anthropologists have observed that the style of the ger in Mongolia was pretty much standard in appearance. Most variations and improvements have been made in Outer Mongolia, perhaps owing in part to foreign influence. Some alterations were also noticed in Afghanistan, where a type of yurt is found amongst the herdsmen population. The names for these actual components, which I mention in the following paragraphs, are derived from the terminology for the ger of the Khalkha Mongols, in northwestern Outer Mongolia.

Several sections of latticework, composed of sticks 5 to 6 feet high, each known as a *hana*, would comprise the walls of the ger. In appearance they would closely resemble the American "baby gate." Just as this short gate would contract and expand to permit and deny passage, each hana would be opened and lashed in an upright position to other wall sections when the ger was being assembled. When the dwelling was being packed and transported, the pieces of each hana were pushed together and stored on the back of a camel. The number of sticks in each hana would vary according to the size desired for the erected ger. Smaller gers might have only 18 pieces or 9 pairs, while some of the larger varieties would range from 24 to even 32 sticks for large ceremonial "halls."

The size of the ger would also vary as the number of wall sections were increased or diminished. The average Mongol household would have a 4-hana ger, while the wealthier members of the community and some lama priests might have 6-, 8-, or even 12-hana gers. One begins to recognize the yurt's flexibility by recalling a few interesting accounts that I came by in the course of research. In 1927, in Ulan Bator, the capital city, a small People's University was started and dormitory accommodations were actually large yurts. But perhaps the most amazing story that I read of was the construction of a 16-hana yurt which had been erected for a large gathering. According to this report, the ger was so large that a loaded camel was able to walk through the door and six hundred people attended the meeting, only partially filling the yurt.* Makes you wonder if Barnum and Bailey know about yurts!!

In order to complete the circular wall, a door and frame were hinged to the wall and a wooden board about one foot high acted as a threshold.

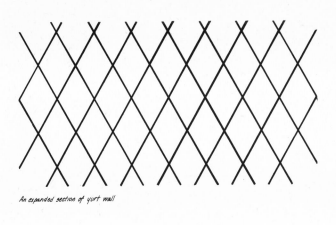

An expanded section of yurt wall

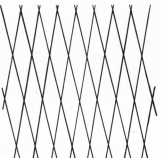

Shrunken hana ready for transport

---

*Herbert Harold Vreeland, *Mongol Community and Kinship Structure*, note 39, p. 45.

According to custom, it was bad luck and in poor taste to kick or touch the threshold upon entering or departing from a yurt. The door, known as a *haalga*, was a paneled piece, distinctively colored with bright inlaid patterns on front and back. In addition, a felt flap would be hung over the entrance and put into use when the door was left open during the day.

I have come in contact with two different arrangements for the joining of the roof pieces (called *uni*) and the crown or smoke-hole frame (*tooni*). In the first case, which would probably be considered the more basic design, the roof pieces were singular strips of wood, either straight or slightly curved downward, usually brightly colored, tapered at one end and looped at the other. The tapered end would fit into the crown, which was shaped like a saucer and was about 4 feet in diameter. The hoop would be socketed on its outer rim and it would fit over the top of the wall pieces.

The alternative configuration was a bit more sophisticated, most likely the type of innovation that I mentioned earlier. In this case, the slots of the crown would hold *hinged* sticks. These sticks could either radiate out to meet the wall, or collapse, not unlike the ribs of an umbrella, for transport. In both instances the number of roof pieces would correspond to the number in the wall hana, supplemented by four to six extra pieces suspended between the door and the crown.

The Mongolian herdsman is not usually viewed as being someone well versed in the art of woodworking. His vocation simply did not demand this of him. He would therefore depend on the inhabitants of the forested mountain areas, whose daily exposure to wood naturally enabled them to be fine carpenters. One item in the yurt's design that the nomad could not produce himself was the crown, since it required a high degree of skill in bending and shaping. This circular wooden frame was filled with inner braces for support. We will also learn that these bridge strips held a certain amount of religious significance.

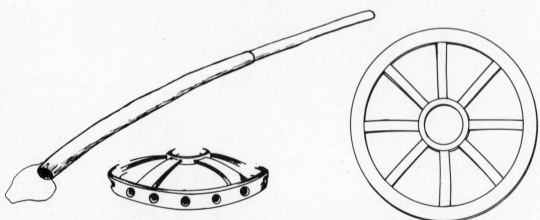

This then was the design for the superstructure of the traditional, portable yurt. More permanent models, which are often seen in the urban settings, would have wooden floors and foundations, similar to those that will be described in later chapters. These stationary dwellings might also be made from harder, heavier varieties of wood.

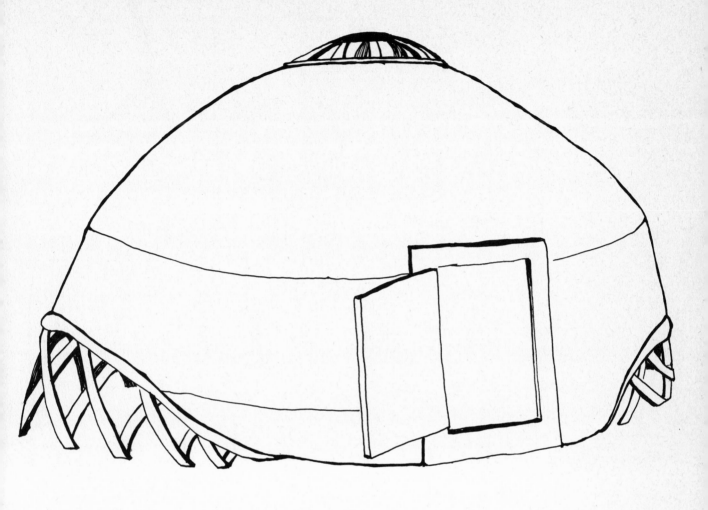

The Interior of the Mongol Yurt

The diagram on page 10 shows the interior of a wealthy family's yurt as it was set up by the Khalkha Mongols. Directly opposite the entranceway in the back of the yurt was the altar or shrine box. No more elaborate than a high wooden box or table, this platform would house lama statues and images as well as a variety of offering trays. In other places around the yurt there were racks for metal utensils, several boxes for clothing, plus a storage bin for boots and shoes. Of special curiosity was the large skin of a cow, which was used to store a variety of milks from yaks, sheep, or horses.

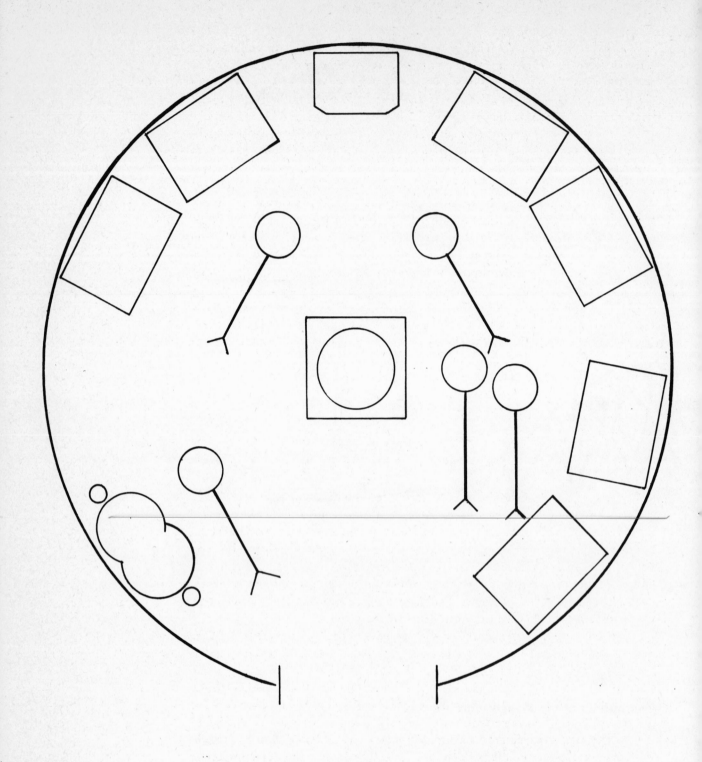

THE MONGOLIAN YURT

Reprinted with permission from Herbert Harold Vreeland, III, *Mongol Community and Kinship Structure*. New Haven, Conn: Human Relations Area Files Press, 1962.

As is seen from the diagram, all members of the yurt household slept with their heads toward the altar and their feet toward the door. There was no prescribed positioning for different tents of the family, except for the head of the family, whose yurt was situated in the place of honor—to the right front of the camp and facing south.

There are many gestures of courtesy that are employed in the traditional Mongol household. It has already been mentioned that it is impolite to touch the threshold upon entering the yurt. The customary manner of sitting is to kneel on the right knee with the other knee up. Many a Western visitor has found that it takes time before he is comfortable in this position. A sign of congeniality, both inside and outside the home, is for two people to exchange snuffboxes upon meeting. Neither party is expected to test the quality of the contents—it is purely a process of mutual admiration. In other gers it is customary for the guest to inquire of the host about his health, the well-being of his family, the state of his livestock, and the quality of the grass for his herds. To each of these questions, the host is expected to answer yes, despite any maladies that might be plaguing him. A yurt in the Mongolian countryside is not only appealing to the eye, for it seems after reading about their inhabitants that the yurt maintains the Mongolian tradition of hospitality as well. In many remote areas of Mongolia, a traveler can come upon an empty yurt, unattended by its occupants and still find that food and drink have been left for him to enjoy—on the yurt, of course!

The Religious Significance of the Mongol Yurt

When the shape of the yurt was originally devised, it is doubtful that this design was chosen for any other reason than its utilitarian characteristics. Such features as its circularity demonstrated sensible engineering, considering the ease of heating and protection against strong winds, while the built-in hole at the top allowed the smoke from the fire to leave the yurt effortlessly. But somewhere along the way, these nomadic, desert people who relied so heavily on the natural elements, began to recognize the symbolic connection between these simple dwellings and the larger universe.

For the yurt dweller alone in the desert, tending his animals and living his solitary existence, the world was a giant dome, at the top of which he found the bright sun. When he returned to his yurt he noticed that this was in fact the shape of his home. Light would come pouring through the opening atop his yurt, further proof that there was a connection between his small shelter and the outside world. These general impressions about the symbolism of his home led to actual modifications to accommodate this resemblance. The smokehole was later known as the "Sun Gate" and the "Sky Door," and even the inner braces enhanced this idea. Schuyler Cammann, a professor at the University of Pennsylvania, noticed on one of his trips through Mongolia that the eight-spoked inner braces of the crown were similar to the eight-spoked "Wheel of the Law," a design often seen on the roofs of Buddhist temples. According to ancient Asiatic custom, this originally symbolized the Sun Wheel, and it appeared to him that the presence of the eight-spoked design in the yurt's crown was an extension of this idea. On the outside of the yurt, an extra piece of felt or heavy cloth was added to utilize the wind to draw the smoke from the yurt as well as close off the hole during inclement weather (similar in design to the flap in the American Indian tepee). Professor Cammann also found that this extra piece had an ornamentation similar to the Chinese "cloud collar," an ancient symbol found on cosmic diagrams in China as early as 200 B.C.

Two designs for the Chinese "cloud collar"

The diagram on page 10 shows that in the center of the floor was a square fire pit. In every Mongol yurt this was the standard design. The flames came to symbolize the gate to the Underworld while the components of the pit itself each held a special meaning as well. According to old Asiatic tradition, the five main elements of the cosmos were fire, wood, earth, metal, and water. These items were all contained in the hearth on the floor. The square-shaped frame was wood and sat on the earthen floor. The fire was always going inside, whether it was being used for cooking or heat. A heavy metal pot would sit on an iron grate, the pot usually filled with water or some other liquid. Even today, where most of this significance has been all but forgotten, it is still forbidden for anyone to set anything inside the hearth. As the smoke coiled its way out of the yurt, it resembled a trunk of a tree and this tree was known as the "World Tree" moving from earth to heaven. Each morning an offering was made by pouring tea on the iron grate, the vapor moving along with the smoke to God. Another example of this symbolism was that the lama priest or shaman would sometimes climb a ladder to the smoke hole and return with an omen or message from above.

But things are changing throughout modern Mongolia, and unfortunately, as was intimated earlier, the yurt's importance and traditional value is deteriorating considerably. Although yurts are still the popular form of housing in the small, more isolated rural districts, and are still found in great numbers in certain urban areas,* they are slowly being replaced by rows and

*Ulan Bator, the capital city of a quarter-million people, claims to have nearly fifty thousand people living in yurts.

blocks of square wooden houses as well as large concrete-and-brick apartment houses. Oftentimes the large crown at the top of the yurt no longer serves as a smoke hole. Instead, electric cables are lowered into the yurt, bringing power for stoves, radios, and televisions. Whereas before, rows of dried yak-dung and sheep-dung bricks would surround the yurt, awaiting their turn to provide heat in the central fire; now perhaps the only thing that waits outside to be used is a small motorscooter.

As the Mongolian government attempts to modernize and industrialize the country, the yurt will be displaced gradually. The yurt is a symbol of wandering, nomadic existence, yet the government's policy is to stabilize the population. In their eyes, fixed buildings are more suitable for homes and schools. Heat, electricity, piped water, and indoor plumbing are more appropriate for a modern economy and certainly the majority of the people in the cities look forward to these conveniences. One cannot and should not make a value judgment for a government and for masses of people in another culture who choose to live in concrete and square wooden houses, yet I cannot help but smile and empathize with the old Mongol herdsman, who came upon a modern city where wooden shacks were being erected and the yurts were being disassembled, and commented, "It is a sick Mongolian who thinks a cabin is a home."

CHAPTER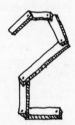

George handed the binoculars to his hunting partner with a look of grave concern. "I don't know about you Roy, but I don't like the looks of it. I don't like it one bit."

"Just hold on George, we'll go over there and take a closer look. After all, Omar's a bit strange at times, but he usually has a pretty good idea of what he's doing. And I don't suppose there's any way that one of those things could be built or hauled in here without his not knowin' 'bout it. I mean they'd have to bring it in crossed his land, wouldn't they?"

"Not necessarily."

"What do you mean not necessarily? His dog'd bark and raise hell if he saw that thing bein' pulled in."

"Now hold on Roy, you just made your first mistake. You're assumin' that they built it here or towed it in crossed his land. Aren't you forgettin' one possibility? Aren't you overlookin' the possibility that maybe they didn't haul it in at all? I mean, look at it Roy, what does it look like to you? I know what it looks like to me and I'll tell you something else. That thing was flown over here and landed on that spot. That's what I think. And I'll bet you Omar Mulks doesn't even know it's here."

Yurts in America!

The idea of the yurt for use in the United States as an alternative human dwelling was introduced by a fellow by the name of Bill Coperthwaite. In 1962, at a time when very few Westerners had ever heard of a yurt, let alone lived in one, Bill was a teacher at the Meeting School in Rindge, New Hampshire. While searching for practical projects to interest four students who enjoyed math but found the old courses inadequate and unchallenging, he came upon an article in the March 1962 *National Geographic*. Written by none other than Justice William O. Douglas of the U.S. Supreme Court, it described his travels as a civilian through Mongolia. Among the illustrations accompanying the text were several of the portable felt tents employed by the nomadic population. Coperthwaite, who had always been fascinated with the space potential of circular structures, decided that he and his students would build a yurt, attempting to see, at the same time, whether they could improve upon the Mongolian design. The project evolved into a genuine learning adventure, whereby teacher and student were tackling common problems together and able to see tangible proof come of their efforts. Perhaps what was more important was that these young people were shown by Bill that they could, in fact, shape their environment—not abrasively confront their surroundings, as was so often the case in modern life—but rather by using their minds, their hands, and natural materials, select a home *they* were comfortable in, and take pride in their craftsmanship as well. For someone who has never been through this experience, it is difficult to recognize and appreciate its significance. Yet, suffice it to say that it is perhaps one of the best ways to move forward and grow as a student.

Once Bill had succeeded in his first project, he continued to look for ways to make the yurt a more durable structure. Looking at the pictures of the Mongolian gers, one notices that the walls were vertical or perhaps even slanted slightly toward the center of the circle. One of the first revisions devised by Coperthwaite was to slope the walls gently outward, realizing that this would increase the rigidity of the yurt and subsequently offer greater strength. In addition, he and his students discovered a way to eliminate the heavy center crown, using the roof pieces themselves to create a self-supporting tension ring at the top of the roof. The structure at this point is basically the yurt whose plans are contained in this book, aside from some improvements that have come about through the experimentation of other yurt dwellers since.

Yurt design is constantly evolving for Bill Coperthwaite, but as hard as it is to keep up with him, as the plans for his yurts change often, one thing remains the same. More important than the actual structure is the idea that yurts serve as a vehicle to demonstrate to people that they still have the ability to create for themselves the kind of environment that they feel most comfortable in, and it is not necessary to spend a great deal of money to accomplish this. Thus, the actual structure might not look the same, and indeed there is a certain amount of disagreement among those of us who experiment and seek improvement as to what is the best route to travel in this regard—but the concept behind the yurt is always the same. Hopefully, your motives for reading this book and going out to build a yurt also coincide, for if they do not, you shall soon discover that, unbeknownst to you, I have secretly built in factors to the yurt-building formula that will cause you to fail. These factors are things like perseverance, pride in craftsmanship, being willing and able to work with others and teach them as well—the list is endless, yet if you miss one, you miss them all.

Yurt Alternatives—Plans

I suspect that I have made it clear to the reader that I do not claim to be the inventor of this set of plans. It is true, I have attempted to include hints and minor improvements that I have experienced, but the plans were being utilized long before I came upon the yurt idea. It is simply a case of my having some time to put into drawing them up and providing them for you.

The yurt is a flexible structure—one open to revision and alteration—and it is only right to tell you of the options you have to work with, besides the plans included here.

I have recently spoken with Chuck Cox, a former student of Bill Coperthwaite's, who now also teaches at the Meeting School. He will soon release his own set of guides and blueprints for the original, portable yurt. His

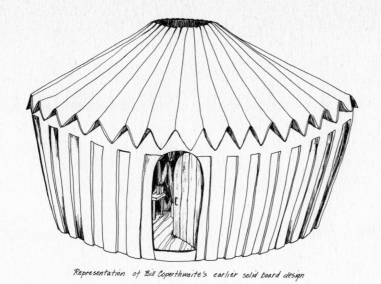

Representation of Bill Coperthwaite's earlier solid board design

experience with this design is extensive, his craftsmanship and knowledge are beyond reproach, and I look forward to the release of these long awaited and needed plans. His address can be found at the back of the book.

On the other hand, should you want to learn more about the ideas behind solid yurt design, you should contact Bill Coperthwaite. My advice to you would be to wait another week or so before you order them, because if you send for them now, you'll probably find that he's since come out with a newer set of plans and yours will already be outdated. His mind is constantly conjuring up bigger and better things and it's great sport trying to keep up with him.

Let me give you some idea of what Bill has done. Besides doing away with the heavy crown and slanting the walls outward, away from the center, he did away with the traditional lattice wall. His initial experiments with alternatives to lattice design were with tongue and grooved solid boards. He later saw this arrangement as too intricate and actually unnecessary, moving on to a solid-board configuration whereby gaps of 7 to 8 inches were left between the pieces of wood. These spaces were then filled with additional layers of the same material, lending strength and natural dead-air insulation to the design. I have also heard tell of concentric arrangements of yurts much larger than the original models. Try to get hold of the most recent plans. The plans themselves cost $3.50 and help fund his Yurt Foundation, which, according to him, is a "private non-profit corporation . . . created so that money coming from the sale of Yurts and Yurt Plans can be more fully used to discover more beautiful and exciting ways to learn and grow. The major concern of the Yurt Foundation will be the collecting of folk knowledge on a worldwide basis and the combining of this with contributions from modern learning for the purpose of creating a sound base for a life style which will be simpler, in more intimate contact with the natural world while promoting intellectual and creative fulfillment."

YURTS IN AMERICA!

17

CHAPTER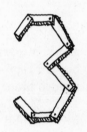

Just as Roy and George were about to go up to the house and notify Omar about what was parked on his land, a shiny 1963 white Cadillac drove into the woods. It went right past the red caboose which had been positioned overlooking the creek a couple of years before. In the back of the Caddy were Mike and Goober (whose real name was Stanley), and Omar's mongrel, Nuffer, who stood perched out the back window waiting to pounce on woodchucks so she could snap their necks—wonderful animal she was. In the front were Omar and Betty, who'd come back to peruse their land and enjoy the serenity of a quiet, fall afternoon. No sooner had they stopped, overlooking 6-Mile Creek, when Roy and George came running out of the bushes.

"What the hell you two doin'," Omar wanted to know, "scaring two children like that?" Goober told me later that Omar actually jumped and lost some of his lime vodka—that's what he was upset about.

"Omar, you know what's back here? I bet you don't even know what you got on your own land?" Roy was always Slaterville's harbinger of fact and fiction. A regular Edward R. Murrow, he was.

Omar managed not to crack a smile and looked genuinely concerned while Betty started to say something about "erts." Goober and Mike were now as excited as the hunters, so the six of them, plus Nuffer, all walked to where they

TOOLS AND MATERIALS
FOR BUILDING A YURT

18

Tools and Materials for Building a Yurt

indicated and sure enough there it was, yup it really was there and Omar stepped back two paces just to prove that he couldn't believe it.

"See Roy, I told you he didn't know it was back here."

Mike just scratched his head while Goober, wide-eyed and disbelievin', said, "Omar, it's a giant jack-o-lantern."

Betty smiled and patted Goober on the head. "No Goobie, it's a ert, a Japanese ert."

One of the nicest things about building a yurt is that you don't have to be a *Popular Mechanics* carpenter. By this I simply mean that you do not require an array of expensive equipment coupled with unlimited skill in deciphering intricate terminology and procedures of construction. At the time I built my first yurt in the middle of the woods, away from any sources of electric power in the immediate area, I found it quite easy to assemble all the tools from my small collection, borrowing an occasional piece of equipment and traveling up to the barn for an electrical outlet when the need for it infrequently arose.

Tools that I list are commonly found in the amateur's tool box, while such items as small gas-run electric generators, drills, and saws are easily borrowed or inexpensively rented if you are without. It should also be made clear that the electric machinery can certainly be done without if they are not available or if costs for renting are too steep for your budget. If, however, you can find and afford them, they will make the job considerably quicker, easier, and most likely a bit neater. Most importantly, an occasional electrical tool will enable you to use a higher grade of materials, harder and more durable.

Power Tools You'll Find Handy

O.K., let's hope for the best and assume that you're able to come by some power tools and a generator if you're out in the sticks without power. What should you try to have in your possession when you have chosen your site and are ready to begin construction?

Gas Generator

Most shops that rent tools will have small gas generators that you can have for a few dollars a day, and this will provide you with a source of power to run the power tools you will be utilizing. Don't be alarmed when you hear the cost per day, and start to compute how many days it will take to build your yurt. What I recommend you do is precut and drill all your wooden pieces in one day and then return the generator. You may perhaps want to rent it once more when you are reinforcing the superstructure. Furniture and other odds and ends can be designed, cut, and drilled where power is accessible, and then assembled in or around your yurt.

Hint: If there isn't a place around you that rents tools or if you are particularly hard pressed, ask your neighbors for some assistance. Chances are that out in the country where power failures are not uncommon and electricity is essential in the home and on the farm, people in your vicinity will be willing to lend you the generators they keep handy for such emergencies. In any event, this might provide you with a nice way to get to know your neighbors and dispose of any wanton rumors about "them folks buildin' that crazy flyin' saucer in the woods."

Power Saws

The time that you will most want to get hold of a small *circular saw* and/or *saber* or *jig saw* will be when you are constructing your foundation and round floor. Again, they are not totally necessary, but they will provide a more finished appearance and allow you to move into your new home that much sooner.

Electric Drill

It is important to drill precise holes in your wall and roof pieces before nailing them together, especially if you are using harder varieties of wood. There is nothing more annoying and perhaps even dangerous than having lived in your yurt for a few months and noticing that along the line where you have nailed your sticks together, the wood is splitting. It might even reach the point where you have to replace a stick or two, which is a troublesome chore.

If you are using hard woods, predrilling is mandatory. If you do not predrill, you are likely to discover that before you have even finished nailing the two pieces together, you will have split the wood, plus perhaps ruined 2 or 3 spikes as well. Since you are looking to use green lumber that has undergone no kiln process, it is almost as important to predrill—even when you are using a softer grade of wood, say pine or hemlock. You might think you can avoid using a drill, since you've probably driven a nail through 1- by 2-inch pine a hundred times and never split it once. But remember that your wood will be shrinking as time goes by and that fire in your small stove will actually become a kiln. As that wood shrinks around the nail, that piece of metal isn't going to accommodate the contraction—result: instant splitting.

So make sure that when you're getting the tools together that you include a *1/4-* or *3/8-inch drill.* If you cannot find an electric drill to borrow, substitute a *bit and brace* or *variable ratio hand drill.* Nonpowered equipment will certainly do the job, but it will take longer when drilling through oak or other hardwoods.

Hand Tools

If you are going to go out and purchase some tools for your yurt venture, my recommendation is to spend most of your money on some good-quality, relatively inexpensive hand tools. Chances are there will be no electricity in your yurt and when it comes time to build furniture and hang your favorite picture, the manual tools are the ones you will reach for in your tool chest.

Saws

Try to have in your possession a variety of hand saws when you begin construction. The need for them will pop up repeatedly during and after the completion of your home. The ones most versatile and commonly available are:

Rip saw (26-inch length is very practical, 5–8 teeth per inch most durable). This type of saw is used for cutting wood along the grain. It consists of coarse teeth and will be utilized, if you do not have power tools, when you are cutting out your floor and building interior furniture, wood storage bins, shelves, and cabinets, etc.

Cross-cut saw (26-inch length again is most practical). As the name implies, this finer-toothed saw is used for cutting across the grain and will be indispensable when sawing individual wall and roof pieces.

Bow or branch saw. This commonly used saw for outdoor cutting of saplings and small logs you might want to purchase even before you are accumulating a woodpile for the winter months. I found that where I was not overly concerned with a fine edge or where I wanted to accomplish an unimportant sawing task quickly, the bow saw, with its replaceable, extremely coarse blade, was a welcome addition. They are inexpensive and have a long life, provided you use them properly and oil the blade occasionally.

Miter saw (optional). The miter saw, a smaller, rectangular-shaped tool, has many finer teeth and allows you to make nonjagged precise cuts. Along with the accompanying miter box, easy and inexpensive to put together on your own, you will find that angle cuts are easy to make, in addition to the resulting joint being considerably stronger. As I mention, the saw and box are optional and can certainly be done without, if you wish. However, it is a handy tool, something you might find invaluable while you are building yurt furniture and if you ever become involved with more intricate interior carpentry.

Hammers

If you're smart, you won't scrimp when it comes to buying hammers. Sure your local Yumongo Mart is running a special on hammers this week. But I guarantee you'll find that your 2-for-$1.59 special will provide you with two minutes of satisfaction, plus a paper weight and an extra piece of kindling. Spending a bit more for a good name-brand hammer might pinch your pocketbook but at least when you're pulling out 16d spikes, you'll know that your hammer isn't going to break. You're going to want a good heavy *claw hammer* when you're working. In fact buy two such hammers so that when a friend or neighbor comes around, he'll be able to chip in and feel useful.

In addition, the purchase of a *10-pound sledgehammer* will be worthwhile when you're driving nails and want some weight for backing. Besides, you'll eventually have to buy one when you get around to driving wedges through those larger logs for the winter's firewood.

Other Tools and Equipment

The following is a list of tools and other assorted equipment you should also have in your tool chest when you begin construction:

> medium-size adjustable crescent wrench
> pair of pliers
> cable cutters
> heavy-duty stapler
> a good level (Get something larger than the smaller torpedo-style levels—at least a 1-footer.)
> measuring tape (20-foot metal retractable tapes take up very little space and last a long time if they are treated correctly.)
> protractor
> pencils and paper
> 8–9 feet of heavy string or cord, or perhaps as much picture-hanging wire, used for circumscribing the circular floor
> L-square and straightedge
> pair of sawhorses
> 12-foot ladder
> small- and medium-size wood chisels
> 15–20 sheets of assorted sandpaper

Materials

The lists of supplies and figures I provide are for building a 16-foot-diameter, all season, permanent lattice yurt. If the purpose for building the yurt is different from simply erecting a human dwelling, if you desire a larger or smaller structure, or if there are substantial climatic differences for your yurt site, then it is possible you will have to judge accordingly and make some alterations for these variations. Hopefully, the guide I include for choosing materials is clear enough so that you will be able to accommodate personal needs and desires, and adjust figures whenever it is necessary.

Wood

There are basically 3 different types and sizes of lumber that I recommend for constructing a yurt. The first is roughcut, or finished (planced), pine 2 x 4's for the foundation. The second variety of wood you'll need will be for the floor itself. Here you will use either slab lumber, if you can obtain it easily, or finished 1 x 12 pine boards grade # 2, common. The third kind of wood will be used for the lattice skeleton. One by two-inch roughcut strips of two distinct lengths are recommended for the walls and roof of the yurt.

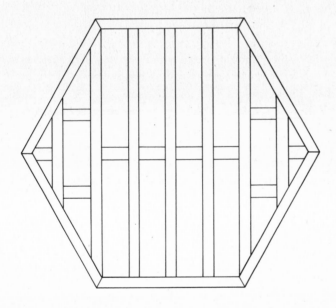

2 x 4's for the Foundation

If you are fortunate enough to be close to, or within reach of a lumber mill operation, then you will be able to save yourself a bundle of money and also obtain stronger materials. To prove my point, travel down to your local commercial lumberyard and measure what is sold as 2 x 4's, pricing it per board or lineal foot. Once the wood has been planed and dried, its width and thickness are reduced to 1¾ x 3½-inch size. Now if your foundation were to be exposed, you might consider it an eyesore to see the raw wood and you might get an occasional splinter. But the 2 x 4's you'll be using are going to be concealed beneath the floor, and your main concerns are strength, durability, and expense. This is not to say you cannot use planed 2 x 4's; but if they are available, the roughcut is a much wiser investment.

Quantity To build the hexagonal frame with 2 x 4 studs extended from one side to the other at 2-foot intervals, you will need approximately 150 lineal feet or 100 board feet of 2 x 4 pine.*

Floorboards
While you're at the sawmill picking up the 2 x 4's for the foundation, ask the owner if he has any slab cut, pine, or hemlock boards. These pieces are the first few irregular cuts of the log. They are the most knotty pieces of the tree, very grainy, and not very salable on the finished lumber market. Oftentimes, they are piled in one corner, waiting to be sold for pulp or other wood processing. If they are sold to retail customers, they are quite inexpensive and worth looking into. There are only two inconveniences to using slab material and these are quite minor, easily dealt with by the discerning eye. First of all, as was already mentioned, they are very knotty. Make sure that when you apply pressure to these knots with your finger, not too many of them pop out on you, leaving large holes. Secondly, the slab boards are usually not of a uniform width, and therefore have to be pieced together to make up a floor for the yurt. Remember that your floor will be 16 feet wide, and then go about finding the pieces you want.

Your next choice, should you be unable to buy slab lumber for your floor, is to get enough roughcut lumber (pine, hemlock, or other soft wood) of a uniform width. These pieces are usually sold in 1 x 8, 1 x 10, or 1 x 12 dimensions. You will require enough to cover your 16-foot yurt floor, or 201 square feet (πr^2).

If all else fails and you are not able to find a mill operation, you can always fall back upon finished pine 1 x 12's. In fact, even if you are next to a mill, it sometimes pays to check out the commercial lumber dealers' prices. You never know what kind of a sale or bargain you are apt to stumble upon.

Wood for the Wall and Roof
The most intricate, certainly most beautiful part of the yurt superstructure, is the lattice wall and roof. Its distinctive design sets it apart from any other type of dwelling I have observed.

Each piece that goes into its construction is a strip of wood, 1 inch thick and 2 inches wide (1 x 2).† The individual component of the "baby gate"-like wall is a 1 x 2 piece, 6 feet in length. The only difference for the roof strips is that the length called for is 9 feet. Although I recommend the entire skeleton

---

*One formula you might want to keep in mind as you purchase merchandise for the yurt's construction is the conversion of running or lineal feet to board feet.
   Board feet=thickness in inches x width in feet x length in feet.
Example: A 2 x 4 that is 30 feet long would be computed to be 20 board feet (2″ x ⅓′ x 30′ = 20 board feet).
†If several pieces deviate slightly from 1 x 2 dimensions it is not crucial. Tolerance for error, however, should not exceed ¼ inch, especially important for the roof. *Note*: You can also use 1 x 3 pieces if they are available. Check instructions to see what alterations in the yurt's design will come about as a result of using 1 x 3's rather than 1 x 2's.

be made from harder grades of wood than pine, it is less critical that the walls be constructed of oak, maple, birch, etc., than it is for the roof. Before I go on, it should be made clear that both hard and soft grades of wood have their own separate advantages. You decide what's best for you and buy accordingly.

Quite plainly, hardwoods are the most durable, longest lasting. If you are looking to build the most permanent yurt you can, then you will be wise to select a hardwood for roof and walls. If, however, you are not that concerned about an ever-enduring structure and do not want to be bothered with wood that requires predrilling every time you want to drive a nail, then use pine or other conifers. If you tend to be a bit impatient when you are sawing and it doesn't appear as if you're about to change your way of doing things, then the already tedious job of cutting out door and window frames will be considerably easier with pine. Perhaps one compromise you might opt for in this case, would be to employ pine or hemlock for the walls and hardwood for the roof.

Under most circumstances, pine will be less costly and perhaps more available. There is, however, one exceptional case that might help you save a substantial amount of money when buying wood for your wall and roof. One-by-two wooden spacers are sometimes used at larger commercial lumberyards and mills to separate individual layers of wood in order to enhance drying and prevent warping and decay. These spacers are often made from oak and occasionally are available to the customer off the street. Explain to the owner or manager what it is you need them for, perhaps bringing along this book or a picture of a yurt, so that he'll know exactly what it is you are building. Don't be surprised if he accommodates you and sells the spacers, providing you with a great bargain. A friend of mine's experience attests to the saving involved. After already having purchased pine for his wall, which cost him $30 and an additional $5 to have it ripped down to the proper 1 x 2 size, I told him about the wooden spacers. He returned from the mill with enough oak for his roof, plus a few bow-shaped warped pieces, which he used as legs for a rocker he built that winter. The cost of all the spacers was $19. This occurred a few years back and prices have undoubtedly increased, but I'm fairly confident that if you come across a place where you can buy wooden spacers, the savings will be quite adequate. Once again you have to be selective when picking out your spacers, avoiding knotted pieces and those that are warped.

If you are unable to find spacers, then travel to the mill for roughcut lumber. It is most important that you use unfinished wood in the wall and roof if you expect to construct an enduring home. Indeed some of the first few yurts built in America were of milled lumber, but the general consensus among yurt builders today is that the switch to green timbers was a wise one.

Most often the mill sells 1-inch stock of a wider variety than 2 inches, say 6 to 10 inches in width, and will then rip them down into 1 x 2's. One warning with regard to the ripping process: You are paying for the sawdust when you have the boards cut at the mill. If the wood is being sliced here, the large blade is so wide (¼-inch) that it might not pay to lose that much material each time he makes a cut. In that case, you are better off making arrangements with a sympathetic lumberyard or friend who owns a powerful table or radial arm saw. Let him do the ripping.

Quantity The wall pieces, as was previously mentioned, are 1 x 2 inches and 6 feet long. To erect a 16-foot yurt according to the plans contained in this book, you should order a minimum of *130 pieces*. This will hopefully provide you with enough extras to account for weak pieces. (REMINDER: Check for knots before you use a 1 x 2 for the wall or roof. If you suspect that it's weak, put it aside for alternative uses. If, after going through all your pieces, you find you are a few pieces short, then look over your rejects for pieces you can salvage. The best way to test for a defective piece is to give it a sturdy tap on the ground. If it does not break, chances are that it is strong enough to withstand the pressures of the yurt. If after going through your seconds there is still a shortage of adequate strips of 1 x 2's, then my suggestion is to return to the mill and obtain more suitable pieces. Often the mill operator will understand and oblige free of charge.

The *roof pieces* will also be 1 x 2's, only here you will be utilizing

9-footers rather than 6-footers. You will need as many sticks in your roof as you do in your wall. Therefore order *130 1-inch x 2-inch x 9-foot pieces* for the roof.

Oiling the Roof and Wall Pieces

As soon as you have all the 1 x 2's for the wall and roof at the yurt site and you have selected your prime pieces, set about preparing the pieces. This is done by applying one or two coats of linseed oil, or other commercial wood preservative, with a rag to all sides of the individual 1 x 2's. This will help prevent splitting and decay. Once you have applied the preservative, set them out in the sun or resting against a tree, in order for the liquid to penetrate the surface.

Note: If you really want to be thorough, you can go through the same steps for your 2 x 4 foundation before you apply the floor boards.

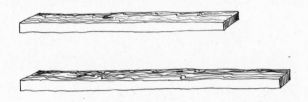

The Need for Additional Strips (1 x 2's or 1 x 1's)

The conventional way to build a house is to sandwich a plastic vapor barrier and insulation between the 2 x 4 studding, with the outer shell and inner walls concealing them from sight. As you will recall from the pictures of the Mongolian gers, the lattice frame was seen from the inside and layers of felt and canvas were wrapped around the ger from the outside. In the case of the American yurts, the skeleton is also exposed and layers of burlap, blankets, or canvas (any one of these being used to hide the unattractive aluminum-paper facing of the fiberglass insulation), as well as the insulation itself and the plastic vapor seal, are all tacked onto the yurt from the outside. To do otherwise would be like lowering the ceiling of a church with magnificent natural, exposed beams. In addition, "building in" the insulation would diminish the actual living space of the yurt.

A problem that develops when you are winterizing and sealing your yurt from the natural elements is that once you staple your insulation to the lattice frame, there is no further nailing or tacking surface for plastic, tar paper, and shingling. The way this situation is remedied is that after your insulation has been applied to your walls, 6-foot strips of the same 1 x 2 material you have used for the walls *or* 1 x 1 strips you order specially for this purpose, are nailed to the top and bottom of your wall.* In the case of the roof, you will be applying concentric circles of insulation from the top of the wall to the skylight. Between each layer of insulation, you will nail short strips of 1 x 1 or 1 x 2 material, 18 to 24 inches in length, to the lattice frame. You will also discover that these strips will provide "steps" for your feet as you work toward the top of the roof. (See accompanying diagram on page 29.)

Quantity   You will need approximately *34, 6-foot strips for your wall* (positioned every 1½ feet), and about *85 lineal feet* of 1 x 1 or 1 x 2 for the roof backing.

Alternative: One other idea that several people have come up with, though I do not highly recommend it, is that they have used *uniform* log slabs of 1- or 2-inch thickness instead of 1 x 1 or 1 x 2's. This may not be the best idea, although it is probably a bit less expensive, because it is difficult to find log slabs consistently of uniform width. Failure to do so might contribute to lumps in your tar paper and make application of shingles or exterior log slabs difficult later on.

*For this purpose you can use pine.

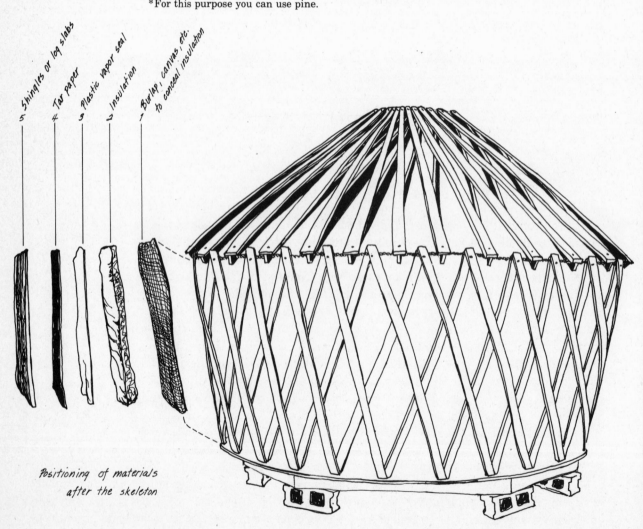

Positioning of materials
after the skeleton

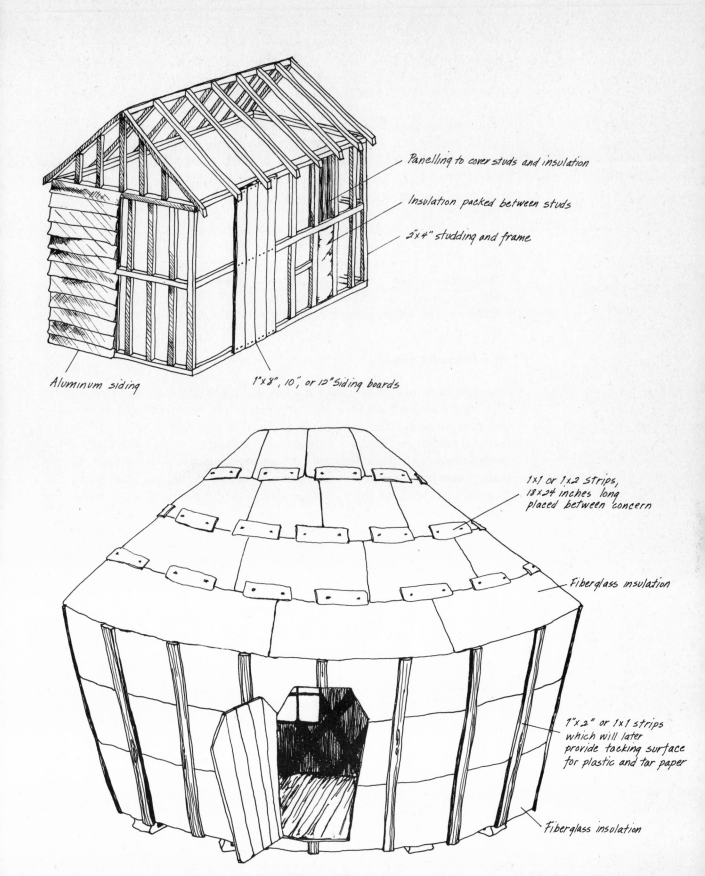

Panelling to cover studs and insulation

Insulation packed between studs

2"x 4" studding and frame.

Aluminum siding

1"x 8", 10", or 12" siding boards

1x1 or 1x2 strips,
18x24 inches long
placed between concern

Fiberglass insulation

1"x 2" or 1x1 strips
which will later
provide tacking surface
for plastic and tar paper

Fiberglass insulation

The Tension Cable

It never ceases to amaze me how young children are fascinated when they step inside a yurt. In a world of squares and rectangles, they are among the first to notice the abundance of circular and diamond patterns in the skeletal structure. Groups of young students from a nearby elementary school were sometimes brought back into the woods to take a look at my home. On one such occasion, a number of second-graders paid me a visit and afterward we sat around talking about the yurt. One small boy did not say a word, but rather remained to one side. From time to time he'd stand up and study the walls, tugging at the 1 x 2's. Finally, he stood for the last time, and no sooner had he risen than he ran straight for the opposite wall and, instead of stopping short, hit the wall with what is known in professional wrestling circles as a "flying dropkick," crashing to the ground and looking more perplexed than ever. Now, since this is not your normal behavior in a yurt, I asked him calmly what it was exactly he was trying to do. "Well, Len," he said getting up slowly, "I'm tryin' to figure out why it don't fall down." Which brings me very nicely to my next point about the supplies you need for building a yurt.

The only reason the walls don't collapse is that sandwiched between the wall pieces at the top is a length of 3/16-inch airplane cable, with a tensile strength of 2,000 pounds. This means quite simply that it would take a ton of pulling pressure before the cable would snap.

DO NOT substitute heavy rope for the 3/16-inch cable. Even if you were to use rope which was twice as thick, you have to take into account one thing: Rope stretches. And once that occurs, what will happen next is quite simple. Your home will collapse and the ghost of Genghis Khan will haunt you forever. So if you are unable to find 3/16-inch cable at a hardware store or naval-supply center, there is only one alternative you have and that is to use a thicker variety of cable, say ¼-inch, although it's heavier and more expensive.

Quantity The upper circumference of your yurt wall is the figure that is important here, since the length of the circumference determines the amount of cable you require. We find this to be slightly more than 53 feet. Buy a few more feet for substantial overlap.* In addition, pick up 2 cable clamps to ensure a tight fit when the two ends are joined.

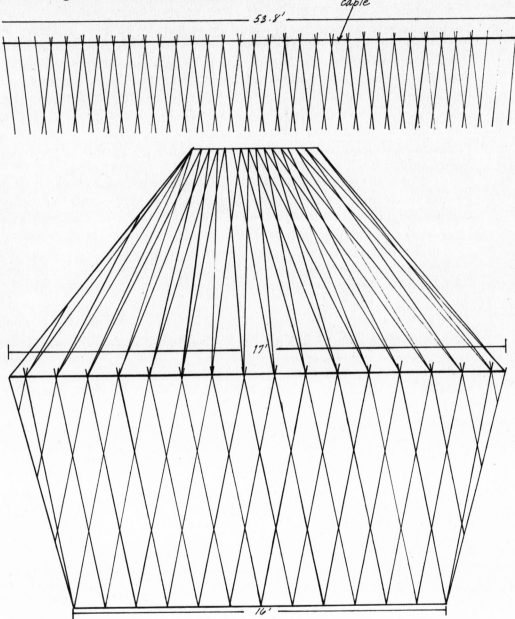

Insulation for the Yurt

If you are building in a climate where insulation is necessary, then you have a few options available to you. Either you can use loose "organic" insulation—i.e., sawdust, straw, leaves, grass, etc.—or you can go with synthetic substances obtained at commercial building-supply centers.

*Remembering from your old geometry days, you realize that the formula for the circumference of a circle is $2\pi r$ *or* πd, which in this case works out to be $(3.14) \times (17) = 53.38'$.

First about natural insulation. People I have known have laid sawdust between the studded foundation, on top of the heavy plastic weather and vapor barrier. It is inexpensive and quite effective. It is also, unfortunately, extremely flammable. Building codes might prohibit the use of any nonfireproof insulations. Check local regulations before you start loading your car or truck to the gills with sawdust from the mill. I have also heard of cases where people have stuffed burlap feed bags with sawdust, leaves, and straw. Again, this is an inexpensive yet flammable method of insulation. Another drawback is that one fellow found these natural materials retained moisture tremendously, thus increasing the chances for mildew formation on and around the yurt skeleton. If the surface below the raised foundation is accessible to rodents and animal critters of the forest, they have a tendency to go tearing at your plastic to get at that great stuff for nests and food, especially once the first winter snow has fallen.

Numerous experiments have been performed with sod roofs, but some people have found that its excessive weight places too much stress on the 1 x 2 lattice roof, causing the roof to bend in over a period of time. Sod may work well on solid board yurts, but I do not recommend it for the traditional design.

What it all boils down to, in my estimation, is that you are far better off in the long run if you opt for a commercial type of insulation. The one I'm most familiar with is fiberglass or mineral wood insulation, and so I'll go into that first.

For the yurts I have built or helped to build, we have used 3½-inch thick fiberglass insulation. Recalling a few below-zero evenings when my fire was left low and I still had to get up in the middle of the night to let in some cool air, since the yurt was so warm, I would speculate that it is quite adequate insulation. You may even want to select a thinner variety of fiberglass pile if you enjoy a cooler environment or your climate is not as severe. For those of you in extremely harsh settings, thicker insulation is available.

As for the 3½-inch insulation, it is sold in widths of 16 and 24 inches. Considering the spacing of your 2 x 4 studded foundation and the desire to do the fastest, most efficient job of insulating the wall and roof, it makes sense to choose the 24-inch width. To date it is sold in rolls of 70 and 108 square feet.

Quantity To insulate the floor, walls, and roof, you will need approximately 675 square feet of fiberglass insulation.

Foam for Insulation

Should you be curious and feel like experimenting, you might want to check out one of the several varieties of flexible foam insulation that is available. The one kind I have had brief contact with is polyurethane, thin foam sheets, similar to the type used as padding in some furniture, also found in some sleeping bags and mattress liners. Because I do not have a great deal of expertise in the area of foam insulation, I will not attempt to describe how it would be used in yurts. Instead, I have provided in the back of the book a list of addresses of places that sell foam and are also willing to oblige and answer questions about their product.

The one thing, however, that I was told about foam, and indeed something I have personally observed, is that it is not the most resilient, lasting product once it gets fairly wet. As you will see, as I discuss the assembly process and insulation details, this might prove to be a problem with foam.

Concealing Your Insulation

If you have ever worked with fiberglass insulation, you know that you apply it with the shiny aluminum paper facing the interior of your structure. The reason for this is that the reflective surface helps retain the heat being supplied from within. Unfortunately, in the case of the yurt, this aluminum backing is visible to the inside dweller and does not make for the most attractive walls and ceiling.

In order to alleviate this problem, a covering material is applied before tacking on the strips of insulation. Here again, there are numerous fabrics you can use. The least expensive is to utilize any scrap materials you have at the time of construction or can accumulate from friends. These can be old blankets, drapes, wall hangings—anything that will be opaque enough to conceal the aluminum paper. The only drawback to this potpourri method is this: keep in mind that the myriad of resulting colors and patterns will be permanent for the life of the yurt, unless of course you intend to strip shingles, tar paper, plastic barrier and insulation to get at the material to change it. In other words, if you decide to do this medley routine for a covering, make sure that it will be some miscellany that you will be pleased and proud of always.

Another relatively inexpensive method of covering the yurt is to use burlap feed bags, readily available at most large farm stores. If you have a large commercial garden or nursery nearby, this might also provide you with a source of burlap. Many times you find if you sort through the piles of bags, that besides the natural color of the burlap, you come across distinctive pictures, labels, and slogans printed on the material, about the products previously sold in the bags. It adds an interesting, mellow touch to your home. I mean, how many homes do you know that have wallpaper that reads "Sawyer's Sheep Manure," or how about a picturesque landscape with a few fawn-colored Guernseys grazing in the pasture? Makes for the kind of place you enjoy coming home to after a hard day's work. One word of caution about burlap: It is extremely combustible and you should soak the bags in a commercial fireproofing solution and be extremely aware of the burlap once you have built the yurt.

Another alternative you might want to consider is to use sheets of canvas. Although more expensive, canvas, which comes in a wide array of colors, offers a very light environment for the interior.

Or if you want, you can buy an army-surplus parachute and use this for the covering. Use anything that suits your fancy. You'll need material for an area of over 500 square feet. When you select the material, make sure it's something you will be able to live with for the life of your home.

A Plastic Vapor Barrier

Do you recall the first time you went camping and you awoke in the morning to find your sleeping bag soaked, and you were sure that it had not rained during the night? This problem with condensation will have to be taken into account when you are constructing the yurt. In addition to serving this purpose, the plastic seal you use to alleviate moisture will be a comfort when it's raining or snowing like crazy and you are lying snug and dry inside.

For a vapor barrier, which is used on the floor, walls, and roof alike, purchase 6-mil plastic, also known as polyethylene. This plastic is sold from large rolls of varying widths, at building-supply centers, hardware departments, and farm stores. You can get by using a slightly lighter variety of plastic, but it does not pay when you have to worry about annoying little tears and rips picked up while the plastic is going on. The sheets are sold in different colors. Unless there is an additional charge for one over the other, it does not matter whether you use translucent, white, or green. I do recommend, however, that you avoid using black polyethylene, since it becomes difficult to spot where the seams have not been sealed with a tar sealant you will apply. Buy a few more square feet than you will need to cover the yurt (roughly 700–725 square feet with considerable overlap), for use as a covering for building materials, tools, firewood, etc. Again, it is one of those products that is constantly handy and worth having in storage.

Other Materials

—*20 gallons of roofing tar and sealant* to be used to close off the seams of your plastic vapor barrier as well as the tar paper for your walls and roof. Purchase moderately priced 10-gallon pails of medium-quality sealant. The cheapest variety is thinner and won't save you any money in the end.

—*Felt tar paper* (medium weight). Buy enough to cover the walls and roof, accounting for 6-inch to 1-foot overlap to ensure a good seal. Don't buy paper that is so light it will crack or puncture easily, yet not so heavy and bulky that you cannot bend it around the yurt.

—*10–12 cement blocks* to raise the foundation off the ground.

—*Asbestos roof shingling* (optional). Use this or heavier rolls of sandcoated roofing paper for a more impermeable roof surface. Either would be added to the basic tar paper.

 —Wooden "Cape Cod" shingles (optional)

 —Log slabs (optional). These are usually free from the sawmill and can be used as a final exterior wall covering. I found that it is a perfect means to blend in the yurt with a wooded setting.

 —Nails and staples

16D (pronounce 16 penny) galvanized common—5 pounds

10D common—2–5 pounds

8D common *or* box nails—2 pounds

6D finishing nails—1–2 pounds

8D finishing nails—1–2 pounds

1½–2-inch wire brads—2 boxes

heavy duty staples (5/16-inch and 9/16-inch—1 box of each

CHAPTER

Could it be, I have often thought in the course of writing this book, that too many yurts will end up in all the wrong places? What if I were walking the streets of Plainville, U.S.A., after *Build a Yurt* was published, and sandwiched between a gas station and a hamburger haven there sat a giant rotating statue of a camel, with 250 sequential lightbulbs flickering around his tortuous frame. On top of the camel sat a slick Sicilian chef, holding a tray with a neon-lit pepperoni pizza. Behind this display sat the culinary palace itself—a 75-foot yurt with the large smoke hole opening every ten seconds to permit the large letters spelling PIZZA YURT to protrude on a 150-foot pole.

There are many purposes that the yurt structure can serve besides being someone's home, and I will offer some of my own ideas on the matter later on in this book. But assisting the budding entrepreneur on Gasoline Alley isn't one of them. So, if after reading the previous paragraph you feel a bit embarrassed, if it even remotely applies to your own situation and interest in looking at this book, and if it perhaps caused you to let out with a nervous laugh and look to see if anyone were watching—in other words, if you suspect that I am addressing You—then the solution is a simple one. Kindly close the book and

Selecting a Site

place it back on the shelf. If you have already purchased the book, try to think
if there are any friends or relatives who could put it to better use.

As I said earlier, I regard the yurt to be an organic structure. Unlike
multisided dwellings, its circular design allows it to blend in well with
its surroundings. The lines of the yurt are soft and continuous, unlike more
traditional edifices and even some of the modern experiments in architecture,
where lines are intricately defined and perhaps in competition with each other
for the observer's eye.

Choosing a site is a very personal task for the perspective builder and
yurt dweller, but perhaps by speaking of my own experiences I will be able to
assist you. I was fortunate enough to find people who were willing to permit me
to rent nearly fifty acres of magnificent woods and fields for only fifteen dollars
a month. If you are in a situation where you do not want to do anything as
permanent as buy the land you will live on, then my recommendation would be
to look for a place where you could squat on someone's property, with their
permission of course, or rent the land inexpensively.

Another suggestion might be to investigate the possibilities of using
land in one of the national parks. In many areas throughout the country, you

are still able to build your home in a U.S. park, if you can conform to building and sanitation codes, if you do not intend to use your home for profit or commercial gain, and if your site will not conflict with public usage. To find out more about individual home sites and where they are still available, write to the United States Forest Service, Department of Agriculture, Washington, D.C.

If on the other hand, you are interested in building on your own land and are looking for guides to buying, there are numerous articles and publications that deal with the subject of purchasing country land and tell you quite simply what is important when considering a certain area for personal development.

Factors to Consider

Once I had been introduced to the aforementioned, infamous Omar Mulks, and found that he was amenable to the idea of my building the yurt on his land, I spent almost an entire summer deciding where I would build. Each morning I would set out from my friend's caboose, where I was staying during this time, and walk a small part of the woods checking and rechecking perspective spots for construction. My decision rested on two factors that had to be closely weighed and evaluated. These were the functional and aesthetic value of each site.

If at all possible, I would strongly recommend you to build where there is water running along the surface of your land. I was lucky enough to be in an area where a sizable creek rushed by about two hundred feet from the yurt. It was ideal for bathing and recreation once it had been dammed with old barn timbers and gravel by Omar and his son. In addition, there was a small, spring-fed tributary that ran not ten feet from my home. I have yet to discover water that is as delicious and clear, and I fear that I have been forever spoiled. Besides this, I cannot impress upon you the value of waking to the sound of water slipping over the rocks or the surge of the current after a heavy rainfall. Once you have become accustomed to beginning your days by listening for the water outside your window, and the sun shining in through the skylight, nothing else will ever satisfy you as completely.

Should you find a spot where you are able to build near water, make sure that you are a safe distance from the highest point that the stream or river will reach during a heavy storm, or in early spring, as the snows melt and deposit their waters. In addition, do not build in a spot where the land is swampy or so moist that you are risking sinking in the mud.

As I have already stated, the place you decide to erect your yurt will largely depend on personal preferences. Whether you select a wooded setting or climb atop a mountain to live, the yurt is adaptable and strong enough to withstand the natural forces you might come up against.

Make sure that you will always be satisfied in the location you choose. Some preliminary ways to ensure continued happiness with your decision are: first of all try sleeping on the spot several times before you begin to construct the foundation, to see what it will be like in the morning. Will there be

The yurt can be designed to blend in with any wooded setting.

adequate sunlight? Imagine what the surrounding area will look like during the various seasons. Will there be ample camouflage and cover from any neighbors or intruders? On the other hand, are you going to be too isolated and will you find your home inaccessible at times? A friend built his yurt across a body of water and found that in the winter when the stream swelled, he was unable to reach his home. Despite any bridge arrangement we concocted, we realized that until the water receded, his home was off limits.

The one flaw in my site, which I will pass on to you in hopes that the same mistake can be avoided, was that I settled in a valley and found that my thermostatically controlled wood-burning stove required a great deal more wind draft than the variable air currents were able to provide. This was coupled with the fact that the yurt was nestled in between a thick cluster of pines. Thus, I was forced to raise my stove pipe higher than I would have normally done, and this solution was realized only after tarry creosote formations on the inside of the stove pipe had caused considerable damage to the stove itself. Thus, there indeed might be a grain of truth to a Mongolian adage I came upon, regarding the selection of a proper yurt site. According to this old saying, a yurt is never placed where the shadow of a tree can fall upon

it, for this brings bad luck. All things considered, however, I guess that it is easier to conform to such an idea when you are living in the desert or the barren plains and your main source of fuel is dried bricks of yak- or sheep- dung.

Checking Out Local Regulations

To be certain of the area you are building in, inquire from some knowledgeable individual or agency in the area about the propriety of your yurt's location. In addition to learning about such things as the safety of your site, also find out whether or not the water is suitable for drinking. If you intend to construct an outhouse, find out if you are too close to the ground water supply and whether or not the terrain is suitable for drainage.

While you are at it, you might as well collect information, before you build, about construction codes and regulations. Although it may appear at first that there is absolutely no provision for such a structure as a yurt, and that you will be in direct violation of existing laws, there are ways to *legally* work around them. Allow me to give two examples to illustrate this point.

SELECTING A SITE

Some individuals who have built and lived in yurts avoided a loggerhead with local authorities by calling the yurts "tent frames," which enables them to be labeled legal structures. My own experience regarded a "second door" policy, requiring me to have an emergency exit. At the time that the County Building Council sent a representative to check my yurt out, I had already enclosed my walls and only one door was provided. At the time that he approached me on the matter, I was standing outside on a ladder that ran from the center of my floor through the skylight, busy applying insulation. When he asked me about my second door, I casually told him that the skylight was my emergency exit! I never had anything said to me about it again. Of course, had I checked into the law before I built the yurt, I would have simply added a small back door to meet the standards of the local zoning regulations.

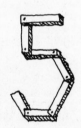

It was one of those magnificent fall mornings, nearly two weeks after my visit from George and Roy. Heavy winds had whipped through the area the night before and all but a few leaves were stripped from the ash and maples surrounding my home. Kneeling on a makeshift bridge, which spanned the nearby stream, I was rinsing the morning's dishes, almost entranced as I scanned the red and orange-colored forest floor. Suddenly, I heard my name being called and turned to see a small, elderly woman peeking into the yurt. Realizing that no one was inside, she started to leave, when she met me as I returned with the dishes and a day's supply of fresh spring water. She introduced herself as the woman who took the local census, and it appeared that a few days before, she had been talking to Roy when he mentioned the people living in the caboose, the newly built cabin, and the round yurt. She had come to register the new residents and make sure that all dogs were licensed as well. As we sat drinking coffee, she admired the yurt and stated that she really did envy me, except for one thing.

"Tell me," she said in dead earnest, "isn't it a bit difficult for a young fellow like yourself to be living in this round house? Surely, your friends have a much easier time of it living in the caboose and cabin?"

As I did not understand, she continued. "Well," she remarked, swinging

BUILDING THE FLOOR
AND FOUNDATION

42

Building the Floor and Foundation

her arm in a wide circle, "I'd imagine that they just find it a bit more convenient to corner their young ladies in their homes than you do in yours."

There just weren't too many times you could disagree with the people of Slaterville Springs.

Checklist of tools and supplies for the floor and foundation

Required Tools

hammers
saws
(a) for the foundation
    cross-cut handsaw or
    electrical circular saw
(b) for the floor
    hand rip saw or bow saw *or*
    power saber saw or jig saw

20-foot measuring tape
protractor
heavy-duty stapler
heavy string or wire
level

Supplies

10–12 cement blocks *or*
6 cement blocks and 6 barn timbers, 6 x 6 inches, 8 feet long.
150 lineal feet of pine 2 x 4's (roughcut preferred), broken down in the following lengths:
  6 pieces of 8-footers
  6 pieces of 14-footers
  1 piece of 12-foot length
  1 piece of 6-foot length
roughcut pine or hemlock slab lumber (of varying widths) *or*
roughcut 1 x 8's, 1 x 10's, or 1 x 12's, *or*
planed 1 x 12's (common variety)

Quantity

enough to cover the 16-floor yurt floor *or* 201 square feet
6-mil plastic sheets for a vapor barrier
fiberglass insulation (3½-inch thickness)

Nails and Staples

8D common nails
10D common nails
5/16-inch staples

Once you have designated the spot where you are going to build and have assembled the necessary tools and materials, you are ready to begin the first step of actual yurt construction.

The easiest configuration for the foundation that I have found is a regular hexagon, each side being of equal length, and each angle between the two pieces being identical. As you see from the diagram opposite, each side of the hexagon will be 8 feet long and they will be joined at angles of 120 degrees to each other. The most convenient, accurate way to make a 120-degree angle is to use your protractor and slice off a piece 30 degrees from the edge. When this is done at each end of the 2 x 4, as is shown on the following page, a 120-degree angle will be made when the two adjacent sides are nailed together.

As soon as you have sliced a 30-degree piece from each end of the 6 individual 2 x 4's, you are ready to nail them together to form your hexagon. 10D common nails should serve this purpose quite nicely.

As you nail the first two sides together, place a cement block at the end

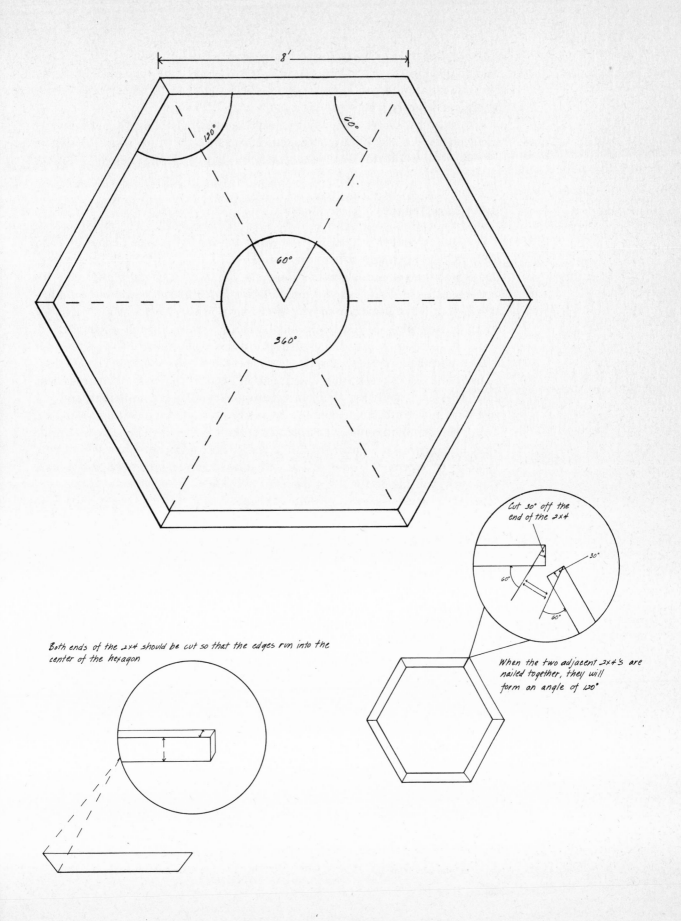

8'

120°

60°

60°

360°

Cut 30° off the
end of the 2x4

60°

30°

60°

Both ends of the 2x4 should be cut so that the edges run into the
center of the hexagon

When the two adjacent 2x4's are
nailed together, they will
form an angle of 120°

of each piece, plus one below the point where they will be joined. After they have been nailed together, make sure both 2 x 4's are level to the ground. If they are not, you will want to either add a small pile of gravel or stones below the block, *or* dig out slightly where the land is too high.* Theoretically then, once you have leveled the pieces individually, as you add on more 2 by 4's and complete the hexagon, you will have created a level surface onto which your floor can be placed.

Using Barn Timbers

One other option you have at your disposal, if you can come by barn timbers, is to lay a gravel base and use these 6 x 6-inch or 12 x 12-inch pieces instead of the cement blocks to raise the foundation. In so doing, you are creating a foundation that is completely windproof. Also, because the underside of your home is concealed, you are cutting off one other possible means of entry for any animals you might have crawling around in the woods.

The way in which this is done is quite simple, though it requires a bit more time and muscle. Using six 8-foot barn timbers, slice off a pie-shaped piece at each end, 30 degrees from a squared-off edge in the same fashion as was done with the 2 x 4's. For this job, the cross-cut saw is not sufficient, and you will want to use either the bow saw or a chain saw, if you have the use of one. Using 16D common nails or even larger spikes, attach the six barn timbers to form a hexagonal platform. On top of this frame, add your 2 x 4 foundation. The only time cement blocks will be called into use will be for support of cross studs that run inside the 2 x 4 frame.

Caution: As you are building the foundation and raising it above the ground, reconsider your terrain to determine if it might be safer to raise the yurt higher than simply the height of one cement block (8 inches). If you opt for the 6 x 6-inch wooden platform, will this be sufficient? I say this not to throw you into a state of confusion but rather to avoid catastrophe. If you are in a lowlands area, or if the ground is particularly soft, you might want to boost the foundation higher with one more layer of cement blocks, another row of barn timbers, or a good substantial pile of stones and gravel, wedged carefully together. I would hate to hear about someone who woke one morning after a heavy rainstorm and had to crawl five feet up, when he opened his door, to get to ground level.

Studding the Foundation

Now that the 6-sided frame is erected and raised on either cement blocks or barn timbers, you are ready to place 2 x 4 studs inside the hexagon to

---

* *Note*: If you suspect that you will have much difficulty in maintaining a level surface as you join together the other 4 pieces of the hexagon, then you might be wise to pour a layer of gravel, rocks, sand, etc., on top of the general area where the yurt will sit. Once this has been done, you even this surface by running your longer 2 x 4's across and checking for uniformity with the level. In this way, when you do add on the cement blocks, you will encounter less of a problem. A side benefit of this method is that by using a nonwood base, you are making it more difficult for ants and termites to attack and penetrate the wood later.

Completed hexagonal foundation for 10-foot yurt.

strengthen the shell and also provide a border and stapling surface for the fiberglass insulation. These cross supports are spaced according to the width of the insulation you are using. Since 2-foot intervals for the braces will afford you ample support for floor boards and 24-inch insulation is readily available, it makes sense to divide your inside 2 x 4's every 2 feet.

The first studs to install are your 14-footers. Five 14-foot 2 x 4's should be spaced evenly inside the middle section of your hexagon. Of course, it is impossible for all the spaces between the pieces to be exactly 2 feet, since you have to account for the 2-inch width of each stud. Therefore, what I recommend is to have the middle three braces 24 inches apart, while the last two 14-footers will be only 22 inches apart, and will actually be fastened to the adjacent sides (see diagram on page 48). What this will mean when it comes time to inserting the insulation, is that the middle-exterior strips of fiberglass will either be compressed 2 inches or allowed to sag below the foundation to make up for the diminished width of the spacing.

Fastening the Inner Braces

Once you know where the longer studs will be placed and have marked with a pencil where they are to sit, you can fasten them to the hexagon. One simple, yet effective, method is to place the 2 x 4's inside the frame at the proper spots and using 10D or 12D common nails, hammer 2 or 3 of them through the sides of the hexagon into the ends of the 2 x 4. Reinforcement can be done by nailing 2 or 3 spikes through the studs into the frame. This is exactly the method I have used with the yurts that I have built and never has anyone had any problems with a weak foundation.

BUILDING THE FLOOR
AND FOUNDATION

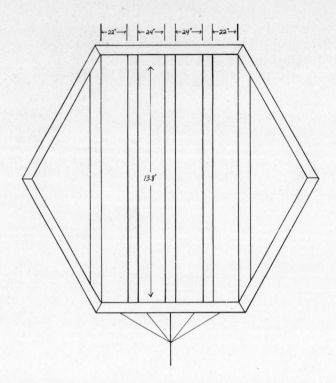

Or, if you wish to try your hand at a more sophisticated means of joining the pieces together, you can utilize a mortise and tenon joint, instead of simply nailing. For this job you will require a hammer and chisel, or for easier going, a small keyhole saw and a hand bit and brace. This method is illustrated below.

To complete the studding of the foundation, the remaining 14-foot piece you bought should be sawed into 2 equal parts and placed 2 feet in from your outside 14-foot braces. These 7-foot pieces should be angled into the triangular parts of the hexagon frame, in order for the ends of the stud to fit flush into the sides.

At this point, you should have 7 cross-supports spanning the frame. Reinforcement of these pieces can easily be achieved by fitting smaller 2-foot strips of 2 x 4 perpendicular to the cross-members. When you have finished, your foundation should be similar to the configuration found in the illustration on page 51.

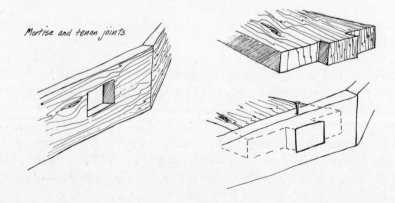

Mortise and tenon joints

Note: Once the foundation is complete, you can apply your wood preservative to ensure protection from weather factors and insect attack. One coat should be adequate for most climates.

Applying the Plastic Barrier

As soon as the wood preservative has sufficiently soaked the surface of the frame, you are ready to apply sheets of plastic to serve as a weather and vapor barrier. The manner in which this is done will depend upon whether or not you are going to insulate the floor, and exactly what type of insulation you are going to use.

If your climate is such that you do not have to worry about cold air penetrating through the underside of your floor, then the plastic can simply be draped from one end of the frame to the other, allowing the plastic to drop 1-2 inches between the 2 x 4 studs. This way, when you do place the floor boards on the frame, you are actually creating a dead-air space between the interior of the yurt and the outside. As you know, this dead air will provide you with a certain amount of insulation, which you would not have otherwise.

In order to make the most effective, permanent air seal, it is always best to have the edge of one of your plastic sheets end on a 2 x 4 stud, and then start your next sheet on the same piece of wood. Your other alternative is to use one of the several quality types of vinyl or plastic tapes that are on the market and apply a strip of this adhesive on both sides of the seam that is formed between the 2 sheets of plastic.

In the event that you are going to need something more substantial for insulation than dead air, then the plastic will have to be dropped more than 1 or 2 inches. The exact lowering of the plastic will depend upon the thickness of the material you use—whatever this figure might be, add another 1–2 inches and this is how far below the top of the frame the plastic should sit. (If you are using 3½-inch fiberglass, drop the vapor seal to the bottom of the 2 x 4 stud.) When insulating the floor, it is best not to take the chances with seams between 2 x 4's, which, although sealed with heavy tape, might come undone at some later date, and expose your insulation to the elements.

Insulating the Floor

Now that the layer of plastic has been added, you can proceed with the application of insulation.

If you have opted for natural insulation, whether the materials you use are mulched leaves, straw, or sawdust, they should be positioned between the 2 x 4 studs in your foundation. Once you have applied one even layer of 2–3 inches of "stuffing," the entire surface should be compressed slightly, being cautious not to puncture the plastic underneath. Another thin layer of material is then poured over the frame. After you have finished, make sure you have left a 1-2 inch dead-air space between the insulation and the top of the 2 x 4. It is commonly held error to think that maximum thermal retention in a

dwelling is attained by having interior paneling or flooring meet the insulation, with no space between them.

If you are using rolls of fiberglass or mineral wool, it should be inserted between the cross-supports, the aluminum-backed surface facing you.
If you are able to employ the paper border that is provided for stapling, you
might wish to fasten your insulation to the sides of the 2 x 4's. This should be
done only if you will not be stretching and possibly ripping the plastic.
Stapling, however, is not critical in the floor, since the insulation is resting
horizontally. Therefore, if fastening will destroy the air-tight plastic barrier,
simply lay the insulation in strips and allow it to sit on the plastic, unattached.

Laying the Floor

Assuming that the foundation has been erected and insulated, you are
now able to put your floor down.

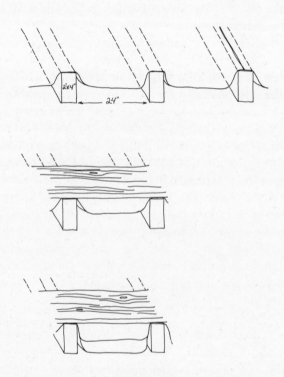

Distribute the boards you have purchased for this purpose over the
entire foundation, placing them perpendicular to the 2 x 4 studs. It is best to
start from the center and work out to the edge of the platform. It is important
that you *do not* nail them in place at this time. After all the pieces have been
positioned on the foundation, determine the center of your circle and partially
hammer a nail into this spot. Using an 8-foot piece of string, cord, or light
electrical wire, and a heavy carpenter's pencil, circumscribe a 16-foot circle,
which will mark the limits of your floor.

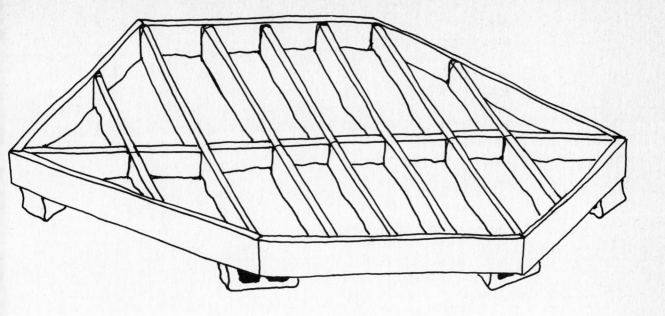

Caution: Make sure that your foundation is completely covered by the circle you scribe and that no plastic or insulation is visible as seen from above the floor.

As soon as the circle has been drawn with a pencil and is suitably positioned on the hexagonal base, you can cut out the circular pattern you have made. For this purpose, use either a bow saw or manual cross-cut saw, or an electrical saber or jig saw, if you have one. After your floor pieces have been individually cut and repositioned correctly on your base, you can fasten the floor to the foundation with 8D common nails.

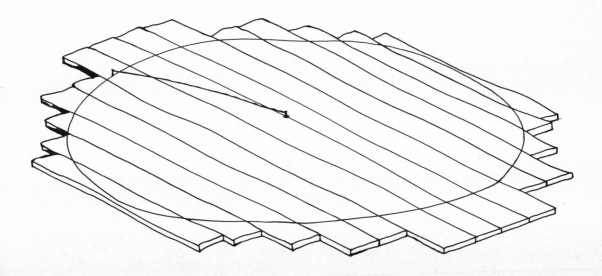

The floor and foundation are now complete. If you want to stop right now, call your local fiddler and dance caller to celebrate the neighborhood's newest dance platform. Or if you want, you now have a giant wheel, which can be rolled down the mountain straight into the heart of town. If either one of these steps seems a bit absurd and too drastic, let's continue with the next step of the yurt's construction.

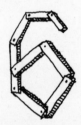

Sept. 11—unusually sunny, warm, and dry—an unforgettable Indian summer day.

Activities began much later than usual this particular morning. Initially waking with the sun at six, I unzipped my sleeping bag to let the valley breeze remove the thin layer of sweat that had collected on my body during the night's confinement.

I am completely satisfied with the lattice walls, which friends and I finished yesterday. Although this doorless, diamond maze of wood and cable is the only thing that separates me from the outside, I feel as if I need no greater protection from the environment, despite the knowledge that soon the winds will change direction and bring cold, snow-filled blasts from the north and west.

As my eyes opened for the third time, I turned my head to see Omar sitting on a log stump outside. His face displayed genuine curiosity as he scrutinized the work we had done. Once he saw that I was awake, he broke into a tremendous smile and soon you could hear his laugh resounding throughout the woods.

He had been chiding me for days, while I waited for the arrival of further materials, asking if I planned to paint a checkerboard on the floor. He had even offered to slice some log checkers with his chain saw. Now with the wall erected,

Constructing the Walls

I guessed that he was ready for the next series of jokes and gags to begin.

"O.K. Omar, let's have it. What's so damn funny?"

"Well, I was just wonderin' if I should throw peanuts or bananas and charge the local folks to come see you. I can't figure out, though, what the hell I'd call it."

With that last remark, he resumed his hysterics, rising from the stump to reach into his pocket and pull out one badly squashed banana and a roasted peanut, which he obviously had brought down from the house. Not to disappoint him, I rose from my army cot, standing stark naked in the morning sun, hunched over and grunted, scratching my armpit and stomach simultaneously.

Checklist of Tools and Supplies for the Walls

Required Tools

hammers
(a) 1 or 2 claw hammers
(b) 10-lb. sledgehammer

saws
(a) cross-cut handsaw *or*
(b) electrical circular or saber saw
drills
(a) bit and brace or variable-speed hand drill *or*
(b) small power drill
measuring tape
small adjustable crescent wrench
straightedge or small L-square.

Supplies

1 x 2-inch *or* 1 x 3-inch, 6-foot strips of pine or if you want, oak (minimum 130 pieces)
55-60 feet of 3/16-inch cable, depending upon how much bulge you want in your wall design (heavier cable can be substituted if 3/16-inch is unavailable or if you experience exceptionally heavy snowfalls in your area)
2 accompanying cable clamps to fit the cable you buy
roll of 1-inch width masking tape
sandpaper—medium weight

Nails

10D common nails
8D common nails

The basic unit in the construction of the yurt wall is a pair of 1 x 2-inch pieces, 6 feet in length. Assuming that your floor diameter is 16 feet, you would be wise to increase the upper diameter of the wall to between 17 and 17½ feet, this figure providing you with an amply bulging wall for a more durable, stable yurt. Once you have decided what the upper diameter of your wall will be, you can determine how much cable you are going to need by multiplying the diameter by pi (3.14) to get the upper circumference of your wall.

Once you have found your circumference and purchased enough cable, allowing for an adequate amount of overlap, you can start to mark your cable with the masking tape you should have on hand (1-inch variety). Starting in 2

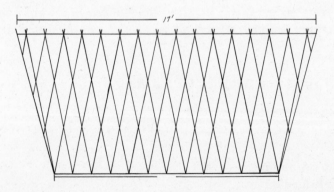

or 3 feet, measure off 1 foot with a straightedge or your measuring tape and twist an inch or 2 of masking tape around this spot. Be sure, if you are marking the cable should be rolled up and placed in a dry location, so that the tape (See illustration below.) Otherwise, you are not getting an accurate reading and this could result in trouble later on in the assembly process. When you finish marking the cable, you should have as many markings as there are feet in the upper circumference of the wall. In other words, if your upper circumference is going to be 53 feet, then there are going to be 53 pieces of tape on the cable, all placed at 1-foot intervals. Once you have accomplished this, the cable should be rolled up and placed in a dry location, so that the tape will not slide on a wet surface when it is put into use.

Upper circumference of wall

Constructing the Pairs for the Wall

Your next step is to start pairing up the 6-foot pieces you have set aside for this purpose. It is perhaps best to make sure that you have an adequate number of 1 x 2's on hand before you start. A pair of 1 x 2's will rest at each point where you have marked your cable. Therefore, you will double the circumference of your upper circle of the wall to find out how many pieces you are going to need. For example, if your circumference is 53 feet, then you are going to need at least 53 pairs, or 106 pieces of 1 x 2 strips to complete the design of your wall. If you have ordered 130 pieces from the sawmill, chances are that you will have no trouble finding the proper number of good pieces. Any that you have left over will come in handy later on, so do not be alarmed and think that you have spent your money unnecessarily.

First of all, make sure that all the pieces you have selected are of identical length. Those that are a bit too long should be sliced so that they match all other pieces. This also gives you an opportunity to remove ends that are slightly split or knot-ridden. You will recall that you are looking for 1 x 2's that do not have knots so prominent they will later cause the wood to snap, and pieces that are not split at the ends. In the case of the wall, it is not as crucial as it is in the case of the roof for the pieces to be perfectly straight. This is not to say that you should use 1 x 2's that would be suitable for rocking chairs or boomerangs, but it does mean that if a piece of wood is slightly curved, say it bends an inch from end to end, it can still be used if you do not have all straight pieces. Still, try to have as many perfectly straight pieces that you can muster. Once the proper number of pieces have been set aside, you can begin to match them up into pairs.

The 2-inch surface of one strip should rest on the 2-inch surface of the other piece of the pair. Run the pieces into a wall or some other immovable surface, so that the ends will match up. Using a bit that will give you a tight fit with your 10D nails, which are used throughout the entire operation, drill a hole approximately 2½ inches from the end of your 2 pieces, through both pieces, and drive a 10D common nail through to the other side. Once you have driven the nail through both pieces of the pair of 1 x 2's, the nail can be clenched. This is done quite simply by resting the pointed end of the nail against a large rock or your sledgehammer, applying a slight degree of pressure against the grain of the wood, and hammering lightly, until you see that the nail is bending against the grain. Once you notice this, you can tap more heavily until the nail lies flush with the surface of the wood.

Note: If you see that despite your drilling the hole through both pieces of the pair that your pieces are still splitting once you drive the nail, then you should probably use a slightly larger bit size. Also, make sure that the nail is clinched against the grain. If this precaution is not taken, then you might find that when the wall is assembled, the pressure from bending might cause the pieces to become undone.

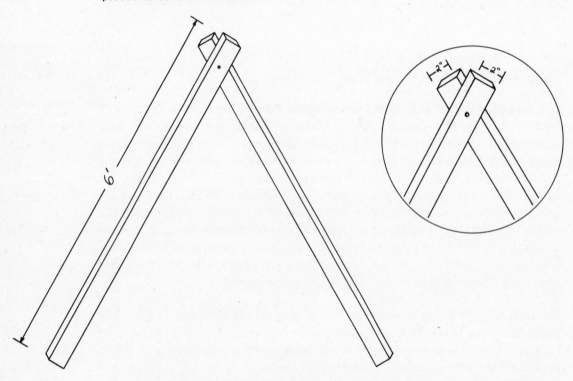

As soon as you have finished clinching the nail you drove between the two pieces of 1 x 2, you can set that pair of pieces aside for the time being. The same procedure should be performed for all the pairs you will need to erect the wall, plus an additional pair or two for emergencies you may encounter. As soon as you have nailed all your pairs together, you can add a coat or two of the linseed oil or other wood preservative you used in the foundation. Set the wood aside for an hour or two to allow the preparation to penetrate the surface. If you desire a more finished appearance and want to display more craftsmanship, you should sand the pairs once you have finished until they are smooth. You will also find that sanding brings greater definition to the grain of the wood. It will make a considerable difference in your finished product.

Sandwiching the Cable Between the 1 x 2's

For the next step in the wall-assembly process, you will need an area of land where you can lay your cable out in a straight line, giving you enough room to lay your 6-foot pieces on the ground. If no such area exists on or near your yurt site, I'm afraid you'll have to move the operation to an adequate spot. Make sure, if this is indeed the case, that you have selected a place that will enable you to walk the completed wall configuration back to the site. This will become more understandable as you read on.

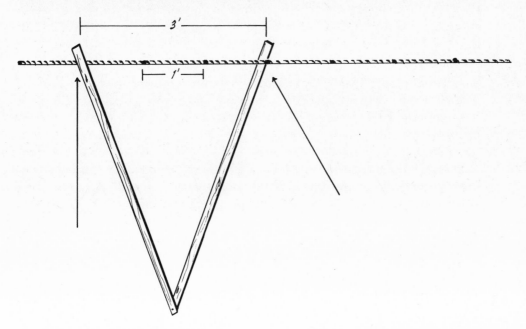

Lay your cable straight on the ground, as close to your site as possible. Then, taking your first pair of 6-foot 1 x 2's, lay it on the ground, so that one leg rests on the first tape marker you made, above or on top of the cable, while the second leg of the pair rests *below the cable* at the fourth marker. In other words, the pair will stretch out a total of 3 feet. The head of the nail you have driven before should be facing you.

Take the second pair and position the left leg above the second tape marker, while the right leg rests below the fifth tape marker. The third pair is placed so that the left leg rests above the third tape marking, while the right leg sits below the cable at the sixth tape marker. When you come to the fourth pair of 6-foot 1 x 2's, an interesting thing occurs. For the first time, you find that you have one piece resting above the cable, while another leg from another pair before it sits below the tension cable. More specifically, the second leg from the first pair will be under the cable, while the first (left) leg of the fourth pair is above the cable. What you do now is quite simple, though before

you actually do it yourself it might sound a bit confusing. Just as before you drilled a hole between the pieces of your pairs, you will now drill a hole through the two matching pieces, 2½-inches below the end of the 1 x 2's, and drive a 10D nail through, fastening them together. The cable at this time should rest *above the nail you drive,* so that when the wall is stood up, the cable will be sandwiched between the 1 x 2's, with all the pressure from your roof, which you will put up later, driven down onto the nail. Once you have positioned the cable above the nail, the pieces should be hammered close together so that the cable can not slip from this designated spot. After you have accomplished this, clinch the nail in the same fashion that you did before. If either of the pieces of wood should split, it is imperative that the piece be replaced with one that is intact.

Your next step is to take your fifth pair and follow the same procedure that you did with the fourth pair. This time, the first or left leg of the fifth pair will rest above the cable and be joined with the right or bottom leg from your second pair. You can continue to do the same thing with your sixth, seventh, eighth, ninth, . . . etc, pairs until you have mounted all the pairs you will be using for your wall, onto your cable. Make sure that each time you nail the pieces together, they are an identical length from the end. Notice that your first three pairs and last pair are not nailed to any other pieces. You will soon see that they will in fact be matched up together.

Caution: After you have finished nailing and sandwiching your wall pieces, check to make sure that the configuration you have made is such that all right legs of the pairs are the bottom pieces (below the cable), while the left legs are the uppermost pieces of wood.

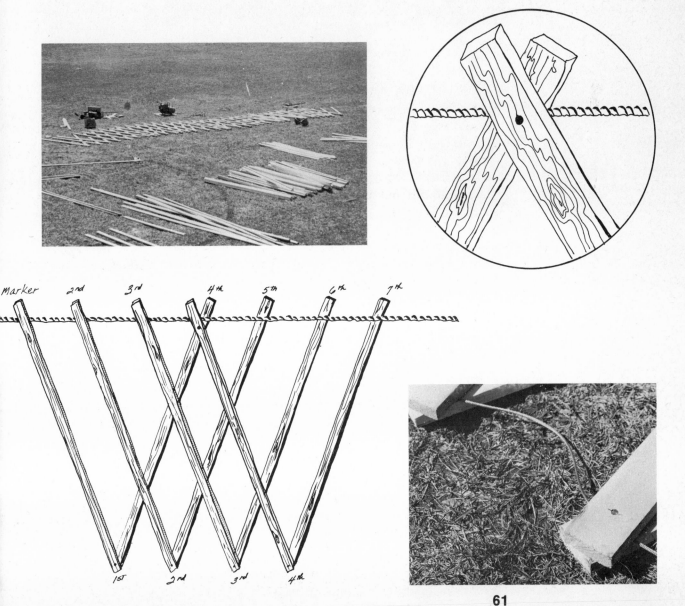

Mounting the Wall on the Floor

In order to complete the wall's construction, you will require the assistance of a few friends—the more the merrier. Have them distribute themselves along the wall "fence," so that their feet are nearest the side where the cable has been fixed in place. The wall should be picked up carefully, everyone raising their section at the same time, to avoid unnecessary strain on

the wall configuration and also to prevent the cable from slipping from its designated spot. The people who are holding the end pieces should also be careful not to alter the arrangement of the loose pieces, which as of yet have not been attached to the rest of the frame. When this phase of the operation is finished, the people should be holding the wall upright, the cable side up and clenched ends of the nails you have driven facing them. The reason for having the clenched side toward them is so that unsightly bent nail ends are not visible from the inside of the yurt after it has been covered.

CONSTRUCTING THE WALLS

Once the wall has been assembled to form a circle, check for equal spacing of the pairs, top and bottom.

Once the wall has been raised from the ground, you might wish to compress the pieces together like an accordian, so that transporting the wall is not as cumbersome and difficult. If you decide to make the circumference of the wall smaller in this fashion, make sure that the cable does not slip from between the 1 x 2 pieces. This has happened to me on occasion, so you should be on the lookout for this slippage to occur while the wall is being compressed and moved toward the floor. If the cable does come free, place it back where it belongs, using your tape marker as a guide for repositioning, and reclench the nail, using your sledgehammer for backing.

Slowly walk the wall toward the floor of the yurt, having the person holding one end remain stationary once he comes to the edge of the floor. The other participants should walk around the circular floor until they eventually meet up with the end person on the other side. Next, have everyone hoist the wall pieces onto the floor and space them out evenly on both the top and bottom.

To complete the wall design, match up your dangling ends that do not have mates. It is important that the pieces are coordinated correctly, and although it might appear a bit confusing, you should have little trouble if you follow the illustration provided. As soon as you have matched the end pieces, holes should be drilled between the mates and nails driven from the inside of the yurt through both 1 x 2's. Once again, the cable will rest above the nail, and sandwiched between the wood. Nails are clenched in the same way they were before. After this has been accomplished, the 2-inch cable clamps you purchased should be secured tightly to prevent the cable from slipping. It is crucial that the cable is tight. The last person who didn't sufficiently tighten one woke one day to find that her wall had widened and that her roof had subsequently inverted.

Once you have finished matching the pieces and nailing them together with your cable sandwiched between the 1 x 2's, you should not be able to tell where your two ends were before you began. Instead, what you should have is an endless, doorless "baby gate" wall. Space the wall pieces evenly, at both the top and bottom. You will find, most likely, that you have the most difficulty in even distribution at the base of your wall, where clusters of pieces are grouped together. Make sure that they are spaced at even intervals.

Preventing the Wall from Wandering

You will learn while you are adding on your roof that the wall pieces have a mind of their own, and will want to move either inside toward the

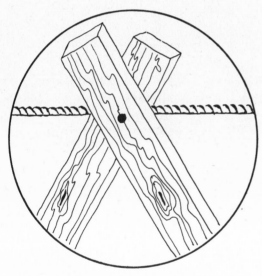

Completed 'Baby Gate' wall fence

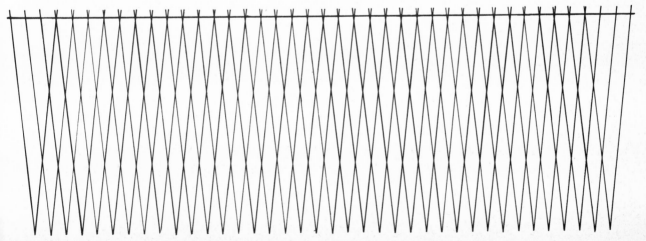

center, or more dangerously off the edge of your floor. To guard against this from occurring, you would be wise to use some scrap pieces of 1 x 2 left over from your wall, and cut them into 2- or 3-inch strips. These small pieces can now be nailed to your floor, inside and outside the wall. I do not recommend that the wall be reinforced further at this time. Nails can later be driven where the 1 x 2's cross each other, after the roof has been mounted and secured.

The person inside the yurt while the wall was being joined will be very quick to point out that as of now there is no means by which he can leave. Unlike the original Mongolian design, which had a separate door unit that was fastened to the wall, the American version does not provide for a door in the wall construction. Rather, a door must be cut out from the skeletal structure itself and reinforced with a sturdy frame and molding later. However, a door should not be cut at this time. The same holds true for any windows you might want to build in later. Most people who have erected yurts feel that it is best to wait until the roof has been added and the superstructure is completely intact. Until you have mounted the roof, therefore, I would say that you should simply

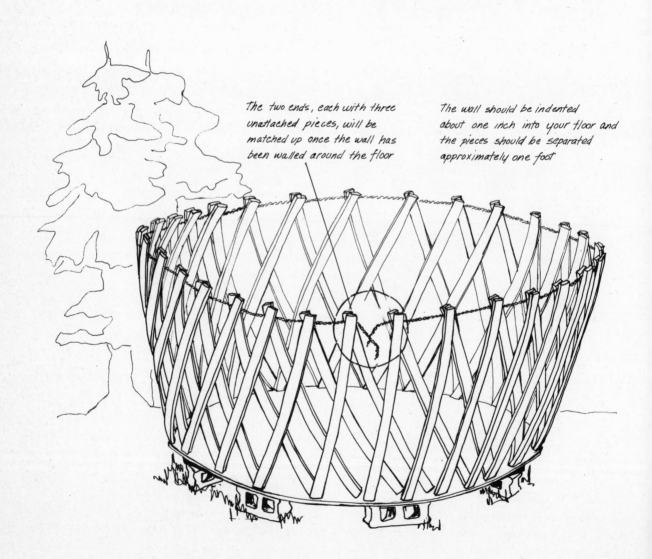

The two ends, each with three unattached pieces, will be matched up once the wall has been walled around the floor

The wall should be indented about one inch into your floor and the pieces should be separated approximately one foot

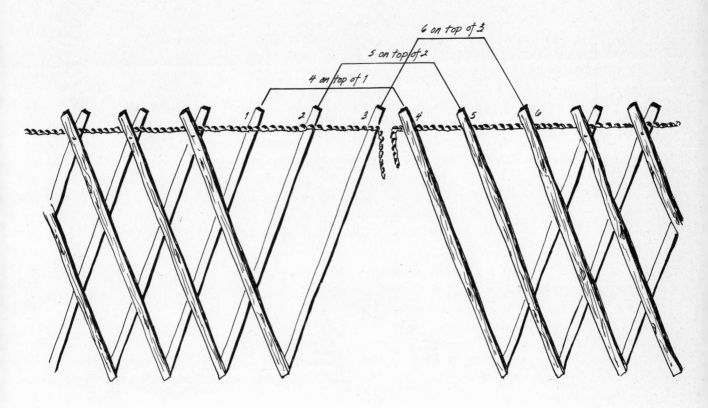

crawl into and out of the yurt when work is required inside, or if you are living on the floor in the interim. In order to squeeze through, you can separate a pair of 1 x 2's at the base just enough to accommodate your passage.

Hints for Building Larger Yurts and Making a Larger Skylight

While you are reading through this book and planning out your own yurt, you should consider some of the alternatives you have to choose from in its construction. As I have already mentioned, the yurt design is flexible enough that it can adapt to almost any personal need or desire you might have.

According to the way I have been describing wall construction to you, you are spacing your 1 x 2 pieces in the wall every foot. Thus you need as many pairs as there are feet in the circumference of the wall at the top. In the event

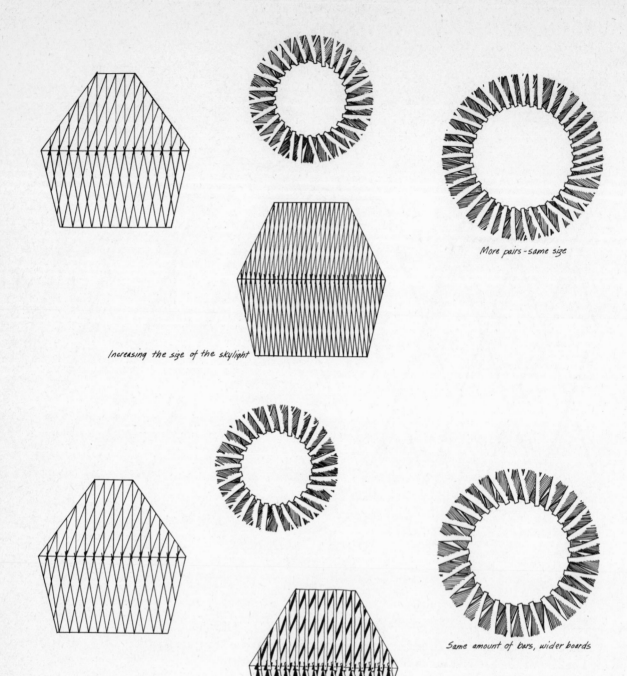

Increasing the size of the skylight

More pairs - same size

Same amount of bars, wider boards

Using wider wood to increase
the size of the skylight

that you intend to build a yurt with the traditional lattice design larger than 16 feet, it might be wiser to space your wall pieces at intervals *smaller* than 1 foot. This would obviously call for the use of more pieces in your wall frame, and subsequently offer you a more durable, solid structure.

Another alternative you have at your disposal when building a larger yurt is to utilize a wider variety of wood in the frame. For example, a 22-foot yurt I recently observed had 2 x 3's rather than 1 x 2's in the frame. Other people I know who have built 18- and 20-foot yurts have used 1 x 3 oak strappings, which were formerly employed as spacers in a nearby sawmill. Although it was certainly a bulkier configuration to transport to the floor and required more assistance from friends, there is no doubt that they now have a sturdy home and that these alterations were a wise decision.

Therefore, if you intend to build a lattice-walled and roofed yurt that is larger than 16 feet, you might want to consider either closer spacing of your 1 x 2's, or a heavier variety of wood.

Larger Skylights

It is also possible that even if you are building a 16-foot yurt, you might wish to use more pairs or wider pieces in your frame. The reason for this is almost purely aesthetic and has very little to do with strength, as I believe that healthy, hard 1 x 2 strips provide you with a durable dwelling.

As you shall learn in the next few pages, the size of the skylight that is naturally formed by the positioning of your roof pieces is directly related to both the number of pairs in the roof and the width of the individual pieces you utilize.

What exactly happens when either one, or both, of these factors is changed? Let's assume that you select 1 x 3 pieces of wood, instead of the 1 x 2's we have discussed so far. These wider pieces when placed flush together at the top of your roof will provide you with an extra inch per pair in the circumference of your skylight. If you are using 52 pairs of 1 x 2's in your roof (you recall from earlier discussions that you use the same number of pieces in wall and roof), this in fact means that you will have an additional 52 inches added to the circumference of the skylight, or put another way, your skylight diameter will jump approximately 17 inches. Rather than forming a 33-inch skylight with 1 x 2's, you will now have a skylight of nearly 50 inches if you opt for 1 x 3 pieces.

Realizing that the number of pieces in your wall and roof are identical, you might wish to stay with 1 x 2's if they are readily available and relatively inexpensive, and instead space them less than 1 foot apart. Thus you will use more pieces in your wall and subsequently more pairs in your roof as well. Here again, you shall find that increased pieces, just as was the case with increased width, will create a larger skylight.

This entire discussion is not meant to discourage you from following the plans I have laid out. A 33-inch skylight is quite adequate. Loss of heat through the plastic or plexiglass covering over the skylight is not a problem with an opening this size. In fact, if you live in an area that experiences extremely harsh winters, you may not want to increase the skylight size any more than is necessary. What I am saying, then, is that here is one alteration you can contemplate while you are pricing and planning out a home that you intend to have suit your personal tastes and requirements. However, when such variations are made, it is important that the builder recognize all the implications of his or her decision.

CHAPTER

October 27, 11:30 P.M. . . . It's been quite cold this past week and I'm getting a bit anxious for the arrival of the Ashley from Alabama. How much longer can I expect the cooking stove and two kerosene lamps to throw off enough heat to warm the yurt in the evenings? . . . Everyone has been gone these last four days and I have accomplished a great deal. Tomorrow I will finish adding on the log-slab siding that has kept me busy for the last three mornings, and bring in the rest of the oak and maple I cut with Omar's chain saw last week. . . . This evening after dinner, a state trooper paid me a visit. Here I haven't seen a soul for four days and this huge fellow wearing his Dudley Dooright outfit, complete with ten-gallon, wide-brimmed hat, knocks on my door. When I opened it I was dumbfounded and couldn't imagine what he wanted. It seems that Molly has been chasing the neighbor's cows, which could spoil their milk, and the farmer has registered a minor complaint. He explained that I am getting a warning this time, and that Molly's actions were a County Ordinance No. I59564, or something or other, violation, and if he pressed charges, she could be impounded and I could be fined fifty dollars. He also told me I was lucky—according to a Farmers' Animals Protection Law, the fellow could have shot her if he wanted, and it would have been legal. He then went on to tell me that in three days, all dogs would have to be leashed or chained, to conform to

ASSEMBLING THE ROOF

70

Assembling the Roof

the SJ874 Conservation Ordinance, which prohibits dogs to be loose from
November to April. Once he'd gotten all this off his chest, he was actually a
decent person and I enjoyed his visit. The highlight of our conversation was
when he commented that this was a great house for keeping pets, since you never
had to worry about animals defecating in the corner. I almost asked him if there
was a County Health Ordinance that spoke to this offense, and if so what was its
number, but I thought that perhaps he might not appreciate that kind of
question. Besides, he had made a good point and we both enjoyed a good laugh
over his astute observation. . . .

Checklist of Tools and Supplies for the Roof

Required Tools

hammers
(a) 1 or 2 claw hammers
(b) 10-lb. sledgehammer

saws
(a) cross-cut handsaw *or*
(b) electric circular or saber saw
drills
(a) bit and brace or variable-speed hand drill *or*
(b) small power drill
measuring tape
straightedge or small L-square
carpenter's pencil

Supplies

1. 1 x 2-inch *or* 1 x 3-inch pieces, 9-footers of top-grade pine, or preferably oak or other hardwood (minimum, 130 pieces).
2. for platform (optional)   2 x 4 inch x 9-foot (2)
                                         2 x 4 inch x 4-foot (4)
                                         large wagon wheel or truck tire
3. 3/16-inch metal washers (60).

Nails

16D common, 3 lbs.

Miscellaneous

2 hard hats

Why Are They No Longer Laughing?

I recall that while I was assembling the foundation, floor, and lattice wall, I was the object of jokes, gags, laughs, and the shaking heads of so many skeptics who stopped by to observe my progress. Those who thought they were being more helpful than the average Doubting Thomas would offer suggestions of how I could salvage my efforts and put to use what I had already built. "Just stick a pole up through the middle there," one fellow recommended, pointing to the middle of the floor," and run some canvas or plastic down to the wall. Sure would make a fine tent for you to sleep in during the summer." Omar was there and his remarks were as expected.

"Good idea, Len, why don't you do that—finish 'er up as a circus tent, teach Molly to stand on her head, charge admission so you can make back the money you laid out for this darn thing."

Despite the fact that not more then fifteen miles from me people had been living comfortably in their yurts for some time, I withstood the laughs and misapprehensions of the people who had no idea of what kind of house I was building. It was not easy for them to understand the roof structure, simply because it defied everything they knew or had ever observed about house-building. When I spoke of tension rings and barrel design, this only added to their confusion, and their gagging laughter would only become louder. Yet when friends and I completed the roof one sunny day in September, the laughter suddenly stopped.

Building the Roof

You have now come to the most difficult part of constructing a yurt, or so it appears to me, speaking from my own experiences. Without any hesitation, I

Cable

Pieces fit flush together at the top to form a natural tension-ring

73

can safely say that more yurts fail because of faulty roof construction. Be most careful, take your time, and supervise all work that is being done by friends who offer their assistance. On one occasion, a good friend of mine was able to assemble a crew of well-intentioned men and women to erect the roof. Yet after the pieces were cut, holes drilled, and nails partially driven, it became obvious that someone had made a crucial error, and it was doubtful whether or not the roof strips were long enough. Although we were successful in completing the roof structure, it was never very strong, and it lacked enough pitch to enable

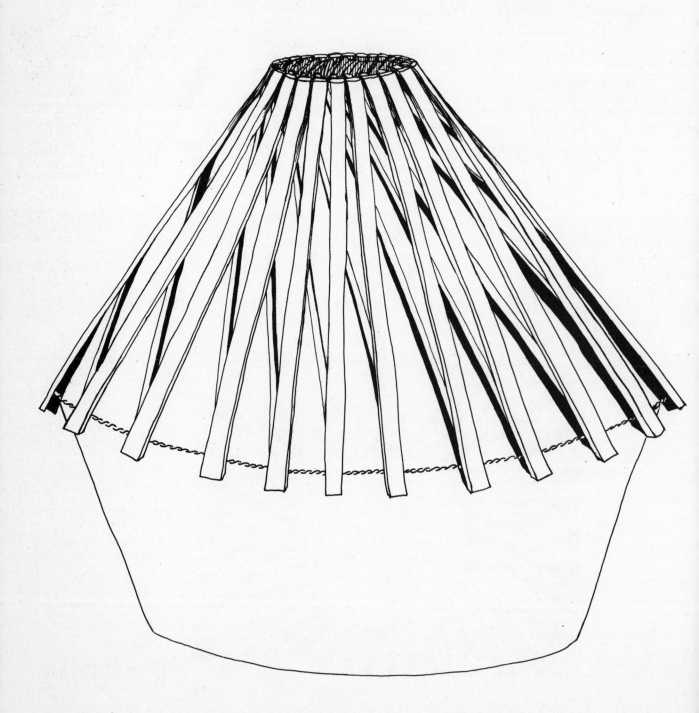

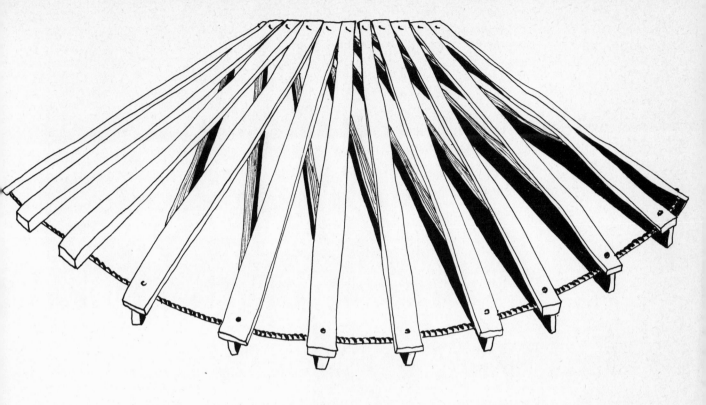

snow to roll off to the ground. After one particularly heavy snowfall that winter, the weight was simply too much for the poorly designed roof, and it eventually inverted, leaving a useless quagmire of wood, insulation, and tar paper.

In an attempt to initially explain the assembly process, let me just say this. What you are actually doing is reproducing the same design as you did in the walls. Instead of nailing the entire structure together before the configuration is erected, as was the case in wall construction, you are going to erect the roof, one pair at a time. Another way to possibly explain the process, is that you will be taking the same rectangularlike frame you built for the wall, and folding it into a truncated cone.

Putting Together the Individual Pairs

The first step in roof construction is to assemble the separate pairs you are going to need. As you recall, the exact number of pieces utilized corresponds with the number employed in the wall.

Using 1 x 2's

If you have selected 1 x 2's for the roof, you will want to construct the pairs in a slightly different fashion than was done with the 6-footers in the wall. Instead of lying the pieces flat, matching one 2-inch facing with the other, one strip of wood will rest on its 2-inch side, while the other piece will sit on its 1-inch side. Rather than having a total of 2 inches of wood providing the roof with what I call "vertical strength," an additional inch of wood will be designed into its construction. This may not appear to make a substantial difference at the time you complete the roof, but when the first 4-foot snowfall arrives, the extra inch will mean quite a bit in terms of greater peace of mind. And when your 250-pound friends decide they want to check out the roof by jumping on it, you'll be able to smile instead of holding your breath.

Using this method of matching the pieces together, the flat piece will be positioned on the outside of the yurt, while the vertical piece will be on the inside. Besides maximizing strength, you will have an extra inch of tacking surface when you are applying your outer layers of burlap, insulation, and plastic. You will need exceptionally long nails to drive through both pieces of wood and clench sufficiently. 16D common nails, which are 3½ inches long, should be adequate. Nails will be driven first through the vertical inside piece, through to the horizontal piece, eventually to the outside of the yurt, where they will again be clinched against the grain of the wood. Since the weight will be directed downward, the presures will be forced into the head of the nail, and it is less likely that the roof pieces will come undone. In a recent yurt workshop with a group of high school students, our funds were limited. Thus we were only able to afford ¾ x 2½-inch roughcut hemlock strappings for the frame. Because of the real danger that the nailhead would provide inadequate surface area to contain the weight and pressure from the roof, we were quite concerned that this soft wood would split right through the nailhead. To remedy this situation, we added 3/16-inch metal washers between the nail and the first piece of wood. It now seems to me that even if you are using oak or maple, this precautionary measure should be taken.

Note: I have been told that for quite a while people were actually nailing the 1-inch sides of the roof pieces to one another to maximize strength. In such instances, there are 4 inches of wood giving vertical support to the roof. But larger, wider nails have to be employed in order to penetrate both pieces and ensure a strong clenching of the spike. Thus, it appears to me, there is more opportunity for the wood to split. In addition, if you remember, the size of the skylight is determined by the width of the pieces, which will rest flush against one another to form the natural tension ring. According to the above arrangement, you lose 1-inch for every piece you use in the roof. In terms of diameter, you will lose anywhere between 1 and 1½ feet, which is considerable when you think of the amount of light entering your home through the skylight. If you are using good-quality lumber and especially if you have chosen oak or some other hardwood, 3 inches of vertical strength is more than ample. The oldest yurt I have seen has only 2 inches of vertical support provided by its 1 x 2 planed-pine roof components. Only recently has the roof begun to buckle slightly inward and show its age.

Using 1 x 3's for the Roof

In the event that you are going to use wider pieces of wood, for example 1-inch x 3-inch x 9-foot strips, then your best bet would be to fasten the two wide sides together rather than standing one piece vertically. The reasons for this are quite simple. Although you will only get 2 inches of vertical support, this will be more than made up by the added "horizontal strength" you receive from the wider wood you are using. Secondly, in order to fasten the pieces together with a vertical-horizontal combination, you would have to use a 20D common nail or perhaps even a 30D variety. These approach spike characteristics, and the chances of the wood splitting are increased tremendously.

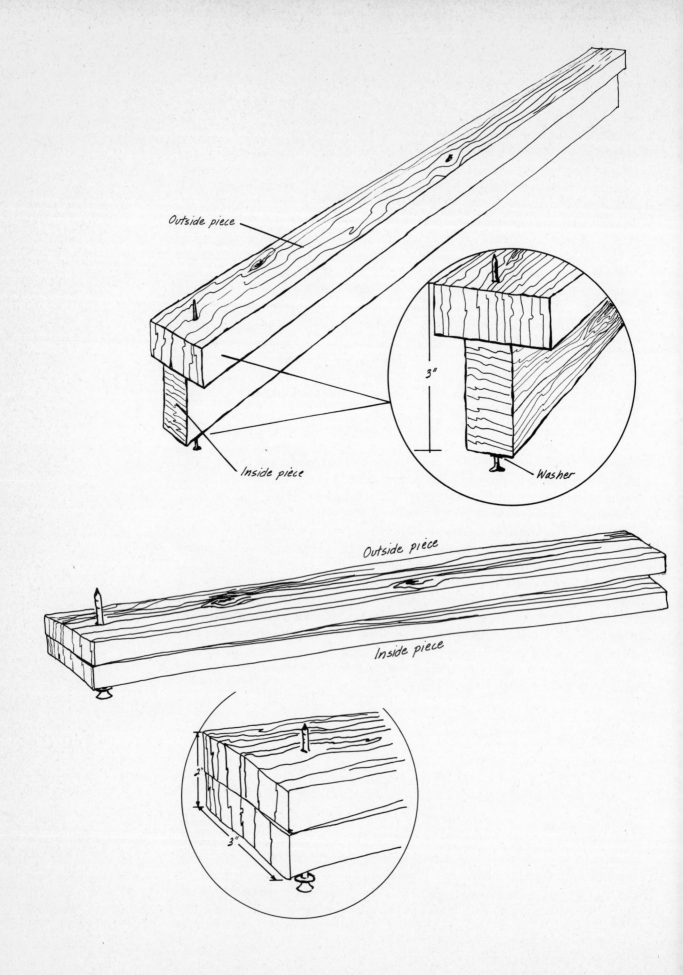

Outside piece

Inside piece

3"

Washer

Outside piece

Inside piece

2"

3"

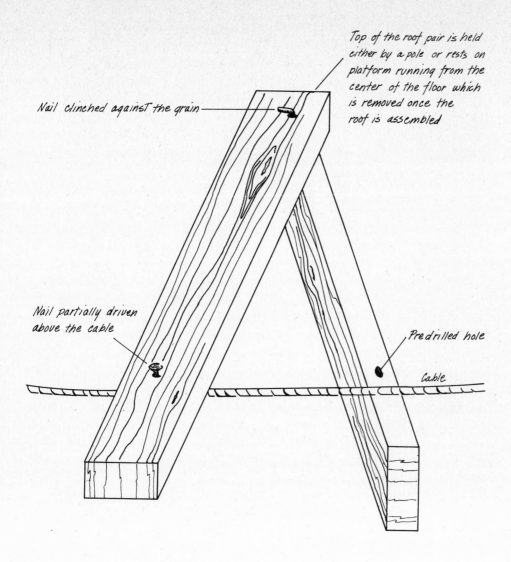

Nail clinched against the grain———

Top of the roof pair is held either by a pole or rests on platform running from the center of the floor which is removed once the roof is assembled

Nail partially driven above the cable

Predrilled hole

Cable

Computing the "Functional Length" of the Roof Pieces

When the term "functional length" is used in reference to the roof, I am actually speaking of the distance from the point where the roof pieces touch the cable at the top of the wall, to the end of the wood at the top of the roof, where the skylight begins. In order to compute this distance, three things have to be known. First, we have to know the diameter of the yurt, measured from the top of the wall. Secondly, we have to figure out the diameter of the skylight. Thirdly, you have to decide the vertical distance from the top of the wall to the skylight. Once you have determined these three figures, it is not difficult to compute the functional length of each roof piece.

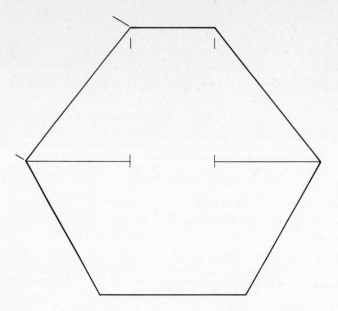

It has already been suggested that the upper diameter of the wall should not exceed 17½ feet, when the diameter of the floor is 16 feet. The diameter of the skylight is easily determined by multiplying the number of pairs you have in your roof by the width of each piece. This number is then divided by pi, 3.14.

Example: If your wall has an upper diameter of 17 feet, you are going to have 53 feet in the circumference of your wall. This will mean that you will use 53 pairs of pieces, assuming that you are following 1-foot spacing of the cable. Therefore, you will have 53 pairs as well in the roof configuration. If you are using 1 x 2-inch stock, the circumference of the skylight formed will be 106 inches. When you divide this number by 3.14, you find that your skylight will have a diameter of 33.7 inches, which can be rounded off to 34 inches for further computations that have to be done.

Deciding on the Pitch for the Roof

If you are erecting your yurt in an area where heavy snows are not much of a problem, then the pitch of the roof is pretty much an arbitrary decision based on your own personal preferences. If, however, you will have to contend with severe winters and your home is likely to be buried beneath a constant blanket of snow, then the rise from the wall to the skylight is an important consideration. This is particularly the case if you suspect that there will be times when the yurt will be left unattended for long periods. I doubt that you'd be too pleased if you returned to your home and found that the yurt had collapsed after the most recent blizzard. To be on the safe side, the vertical distance from the cable to the skylight should be at least 4–4½ feet. You might even consider increasing the vertical slope to 5 feet, if the climate is excessively severe. With this much of a rise, you can rest assured that your roof will have enough of a slant to prevent substantial amounts of snow from accumulating. My own opinion is that the entire yurt looks loftier and more impressive when the slope of the roof is greater. In addition, it creates a feeling of greater interior space and enables the eye to more easily appreciate the intricate design, with its myriad of mini-beams extending to the skylight.

Ye Old Pythagorean Theorem

Building a yurt for yourself is the kind of project that makes you wish that you had listened more in geometry class. But then again, maybe if the teacher had told you that learning the principles of geometry would have enabled you to build your own home, you would have taken the course more seriously. In any event, the ancient Greek Pythagoras must have had yurt construction in mind when he came up with that famous theorem that bears his name. Once you have determined the vertical slope and know the diameters of both the skylight and upper wall, it is the Pythagorean theorem that is employed to compute the "functional length" of the roof pairs. What you have actually constructed is a right triangle with two sides of 85 and 48–54 inches. The illustration below explains the process for figuring out the length of the strips of wood in a roof that has a slope of 4½ feet, with the upper diameter in the wall 17 feet.

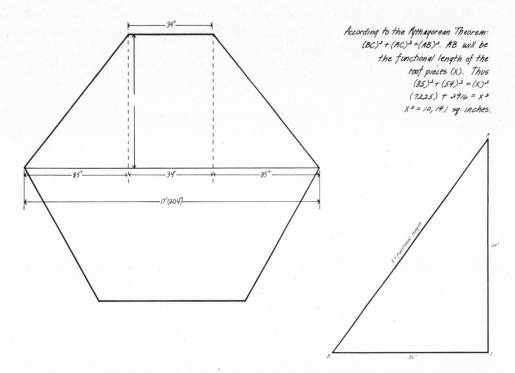

According to the Pythagorean Theorem:
$(BC)^2 + (AC)^2 = (AB)^2$. AB will be the functional length of the roof pieces (X). Thus
$(85)^2 + (54)^2 = (X)^2$
$(7225) + 2916 = X^2$
$X^2 = 10,141$ sq. inches.

Once this is known, you have to compute the square root of 10,141. In the event that you are without slide rule or square root tables, here is the old way I learned way back, which though not being part of the new math, still works.

$$
\begin{array}{r}
100.7 \\
1\ \sqrt{10141.0000} \\
\underline{1} \\
20\quad 001 \\
\underline{0} \\
200\quad 141 \\
\underline{0} \\
2007\quad 14100 \\
\underline{14049} \\
51
\end{array}
$$

We now see that when we build a yurt with an upper-wall diameter of 17 feet, with a 34-inch skylight and 4½ feet of vertical slope, we will need roof pieces 100.7 inches, or *8 feet, 4.7 inches long*. This can be rounded off to *8 feet, 5 inches*.

Cutting and Assembling the Roof Pairs

It is important that all wood used in the construction of the roof is of equal length. Otherwise, not only are you risking an unsymmetrical skylight, but you might also find that the durability of the roof itself is diminished. Another reason you want identical pieces of lumber is that when it comes time to complete the roof with insulation and outer coverings, it is much easier to work when you have the exact amount of nailing and support surface all the way around the roof.

Of course, if you have had your lumber custom cut from a sawmill, you assume that all the pieces will be exactly the same. But if you selected spacers from a pile and have obtained varying lengths, which is more often the case than not, make sure that all pieces have been cut to one specific length.

Once you are sure that you have enough suitable pieces of wood for the roof, and that they are all the same length, you are ready to begin matching up your pairs and nailing them together. Remember that you wish to utilize strips that contain as few knots as possible—ones that you believe will not snap under the weight and pressure that the roof members must endure. If you find that after you go through all your wood that you are a few pieces short, before you panic and go running back to the place you bought the wood, you can recheck your discard pile to see whether or not in fact you overlooked some usable pieces. For instance, should you find as you are rechecking that there are in fact several strips of wood that have a conspicuous knot on the end of the wood, it is still possible that you can place it at the wall end, if it lies below the cable point. (Measuring out your functional-length distance from the opposite end, you will determine the cable point.) Since this is the area where the roof eaves will fall, it will not be subjected to very much weight. If, however, you find that the knot will rest slightly *above* the cable, your alternative is to turn the piece around end-for-end. Here again, you have a greater support network close to the skylight and the pieces are more interdependent. Because of this factor, you still may be able to salvage the piece of wood. The only kind of piece you very obviously have to avoid is that strip which has a large knot in the middle section. Since this is the greatest stress zone for the roof, I suggest that this area be clear and unknotted. Wood that does not conform to this criteria can be used for tar paper and siding backing, support for interior shelving, or plain old kindling for the winter fires.

Nailing

Looking at the diagram on page 84, you can see that one nail is applied to either end of the roof pair. The first nail at the top of the "V" joins the two pieces together, while the second nail is driven through the top piece of the pair until it protrudes an inch or so through the other side of the wood. As you might have already guessed, this nail will be driven through its mate from another pair as you move around the yurt, erecting the roof.

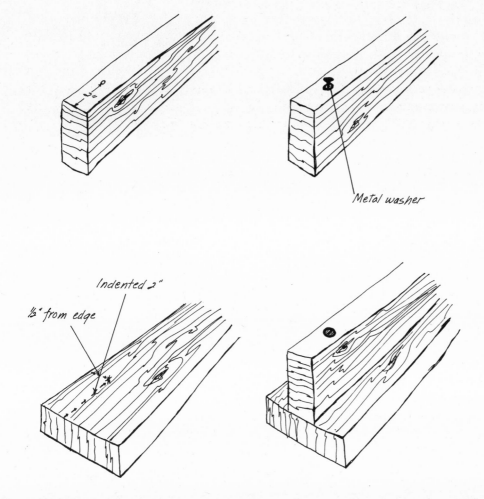

Metal washer

Indented 2"

½" from edge

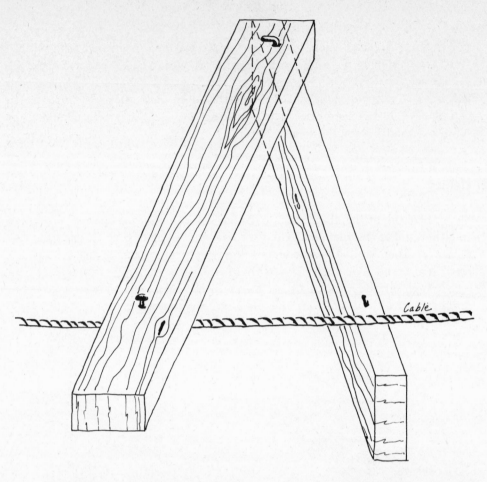

Cable

The junction nail is always driven the same distance from the end of the pair. If you are using 1 x 2 pieces for the roof, what you want to do is drill a hole through the vertical, inside piece of the pair, 2 inches from the end, and drive the 16D nail until it reaches the other side of the wood. Measuring ½ inches in from the left side of the horizontal piece and 2 inches from the end, another hole should be drilled through this, your outside member of the pair. To complete the joint, finish driving the nail completely through this hole and clench the pair against the grain. The reason for slightly offsetting the vertical piece onto the left side of the horizontal piece is so that when the pair is actually utilized in the roof, the vertical piece will be moved to the right, and will cross over the vertical, top piece. In this way, you will get maximum support from the vertical piece and also run the least risk of splitting the wood. The reason for not placing the vertical piece all the way to the left edge of the horizontal piece is there is more opportunity for such a split to occur when the nail is pounded close to the edge.

One word of caution—Make sure that you have your sledgehammer or other solid backing below you whenever you are driving your nails. Failure to so do will only increase the risk of splitting. Another small fact that might help you as you nail is that sharp points hold better than blunt ones, but also tend to split the wood. Since all nails will be clenched anyway, you are better off to flatten the point of the nail with a hammer before driving it through the wood, particularly if you are using oak or maple.

The Cable Nail

Once you have nailed the two ends of your pair together, you should predrill and partially drive a 16D nail through your horizontal member, and predrill a hole in your vertical piece. In order to determine where your nail and hole should go, you should simply subtract whatever your "functional length" is from the total length of the roof piece. Then move that many inches up from the cable end of your pair and this is the point where you will find the wood should rest on the cable. For example, if you are using 9-foot strips of 1 x 2 and your functional length has been found to be 8 feet, 5 inches, then you would measure 7 inches in from the end and drill your hole through the center of the wood. As soon as you have drilled your hole, flatten the point of your nail and hammer it through the horizontal piece, making sure that you have moved the vertical piece aside, so that it remains unfastened. After your nail protrudes an inch or so through the other side, you can move your vertical piece so that onee

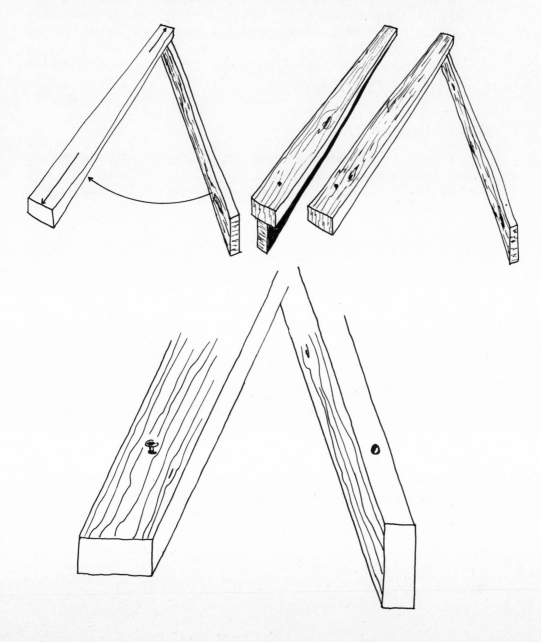

again it rests under the horizontal piece. Making sure that the nail point is positioned in the middle of the vertical piece, you can compress the 2 pieces together, so that the point leaves a noticeable indentation in the lower piece. Once you have made this impression and are sure that you are the same distance from the end as you were in its upper mate, you can now drill straight through the 1-inch side of your vertical piece. In this way, when you are assembling the roof, you will know exactly where the pieces should match up. You will also have little difficulty in pounding the two pieces together, if you have drilled and nailed correctly.

Note: Should you discover that your drill bit is not long enough to go completely through the vertical, 2-inch side, the fact that your nails have been flattened should prevent the wood from splitting when you drive that undrilled fraction of an inch.

Strange as it all might seem right now, believe it or not, you have finished 1 pair of your roof, if it looks something like the illustration found on page 84. Congratulations, but don't marvel too long on your first pair—you only have 50 or so more to do and they have to be done just as precisely. If you get sloppy, in the long run you won't be too pleased. I'd hate to think that you had to take that old farmer's advice and make yourself a circus tent, just because you weren't careful.

Poles or Platform?

In the event that you have managed to keep two steps ahead of me, you may have been asking yourself, how in the world does the partially complete roof stay up in the air until it becomes a self-supporting full tension ring? To my knowledge, there are two possibilities and to tell you the truth, neither one is absolutely infallible. Terrific, you say! You've come this far and now this joker tells you that he hasn't quite figured this one out. Before you proceed to throw the book in the garbage and consult the Yellow Pages for a personal assassin, or start asking around to see if anyone knows of any vacant apartments in town, let me explain. Simply because there is no perfect way to support the individual pairs as far as I know, that doesn't mean that people don't mount their yurt roofs without considerable trouble and tragedy. What it does mean is that it is a bit more precarious an operation than the rest of the yurt. It requires that you and your friends use your eyes and ears at all times—eyes to look for prospective mishaps and your ears to listen for slipping wood.

Poles for Support

The least expensive way to assemble the roof is simply to have one or two people, armed with long poles (you can use some of your discarded roof pieces for this purpose), wearing long sleeves and protective headgear, namely genuine hardhats, stand inside the yurt while the roof is going up. Their main responsibility will be to hold up the individual pairs at the top of the roof, while you work your way around the wall to complete the circular design. You might

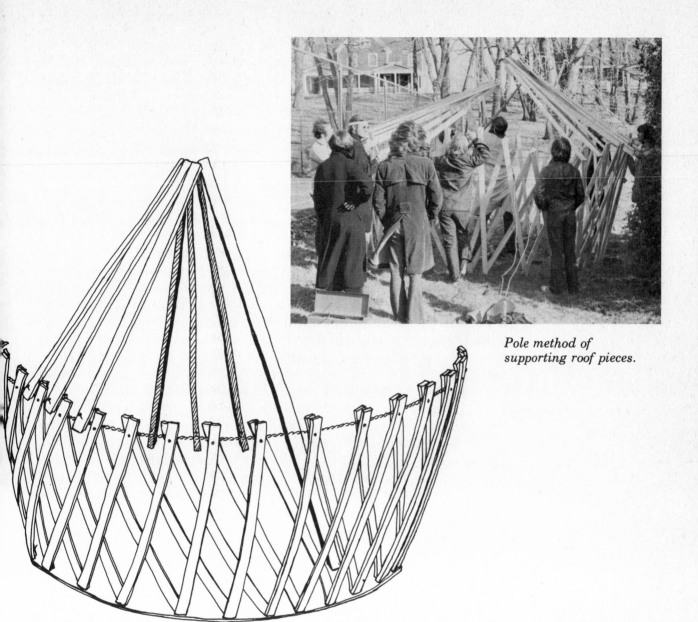

Pole method of supporting roof pieces.

want to have on hand longer poles, which can run up from the floor to the roof, while your inside people jockey the pairs to position them correctly. Comments I have received when I described the process to friends, before we actually began, have ranged from those expressing general disbelief to things like, "My God, it sounds like a real suicide mission." Yet in all the roof assemblies I have actually been involved in, the worst thing that has happened has been that one support pole slipped free and a few pairs came down, injuring no one. My advice to you if you decide to opt for pole supports is make sure you have plenty of long pieces that will not give way under the weight of the roof, wear substantial head protection, and work as conscientiously as you can. You will also find that once you get about half your pairs onto the roof, you've passed by the real danger point. The only time you might be faced with a crisis toward the end of the process is when you are fitting in your last pairs and juggling the partially completely tension ring, in order to make the pieces line up properly. My last recommendation regarding the use of poles for support is this: Your first poles are your most crucial. The source of the tension ring, so to speak, is actually found in the first few pairs that you mount. Always be looking for that first pole or two to slip or move substantially to one side.

Building a Temporary Roof Platform

Since the pole method of support is less expensive, it has been employed most frequently in the roof-assembly process. More recently, however, yurt builders working with the permanent lattice design have been experimenting with the construction of a temporary platform that holds up the roof pairs above the center of the floor, while people work busily outside the yurt, fastening the pairs at the cable. Only one person is required inside to ensure that the pairs are placed flush against one another during the assembly process. Once all the roof pieces have been added, this structure can be lowered and removed completely, leaving you with a finished skylight. The advantage to using the platform is that if it is positioned correctly in the center of the yurt, and is at the appropriate height, you always have a good idea of where the skylight will take shape. In addition, you do not have to contend with slipping poles and the possible dangers to those working inside.

The reasons that people sometimes shy away from the platform are twofold. First of all, it requires an extra commitment of time and money on the part of the builder. Secondly, my own experience has shown that it is at times easy to erect a faulty platform, which then becomes a nuisance, rather than something that it beneficial.

The height at which you build the platform depends on three factors. You first have to consider the total height of your yurt, from floor to skylight. You then have to take into account the diameter of the skylight. And thirdly, you have to be aware of the diameter and width of the tire or wheel you use. If you do not consider these three things, you might discover that the roof pairs will not rest securely on the top of the platform.

Rather than provide you with an exact set of dimensions for the platform, since you will decide the three aforementioned characteristics of the yurt you are erecting, and I do not know the size of the tire you are using, I can only offer some guides to constructing a functional platform:

(1) Make sure that the platform rests directly above the center of the floor.

(2) The platform has to be sturdy enough that it will not lean to one side while the roof is going up. Therefore, I recommend that you use 2 x 4's for both the main piece and angled brace supports.

(3) Do not build the platform so high that the tips of the roof pairs are resting on the side of the tire. Should this occur, you might find that you have a great deal of difficulty in removing the platform once your roof is completed.

(4) Position one person inside the yurt so that he can jockey the roof pairs flush to one another while they are going up, plus also make minor alterations or spot possible dangers and lopsided construction.

Temporary roof platform from 2 x 4's and treadless truck tire.

Putting Up the Roof

After you have prepared all your roof pieces, which will include prenailing and drilling the pairs, sandpapering them and adding your wood preservative (the Mongolians prefer to paint the roof pieces with bright colors), and decided which method of support you are going to utilize, you are ready to complete the yurt skeleton.

Most of the yurt construction process is pretty much routine, but the roof erection is quite exciting for all those who observe or participate. Although I have been directly involved with the assembly of a dozen or so roofs, I never cease to be amazed by the feeling of ritual and fulfillment, so often lacking in daily existence. Indeed each time I have been exposed to completely different experiences, owing to the fact that I worked with different people. All had varied reactions and expressed their feelings of accomplishment in a distinctive fashion as the roof rose and took shape. There is no better way to truly get to know people than to actually set a common goal or have a mutual task for the group to involve themselves in. Whether it be canoeing a rapids, bicycling long distances, climbing a mountain, or building a yurt—each has afforded me the opportunity to watch people unmask their true nature and test productively their own potentials. Few times have I ever observed such combinations of satisfaction, disappointment, grief, relief, and joy so beautifully juxtaposed as in projects and situations such as these. Each time I have been grateful that I have been able to share in the experience. Therefore, my magnanimous recommendation to any group of people who want to get to know each other at a time when so much has been designed into our lives to prevent this from occurring is: canoe to an island where bicycles await you; cycle to the nearby mountain, climb the mountain, and once you reach the very top, rest for a while and together build a yurt. I guarantee that despite any sore limbs, aching backs, and blisters, you will all feel more refreshed and rejuvenated than when you began. In addition, you will have made yourself a group of friends whom you truly know and respect.

Pick a nice day, start early, and have a good breakfast waiting for all those who have volunteered. You should try to have on hand around six people—don't worry about having too much assistance with too little work to do, because there is always something for someone to take care of, even if you have lapses where one or two peoples' sole responsibility is to pray for the continuation of good weather and a strong, healthy roof.

Roof assembly in progress.

STEP 1
Make sure that you have an adequate number of extra roof pieces on hand, in case you should discover that despite careful scrutiny of the wood, a few pieces crack and break. In the meantime, these 1 x 2's can serve as support poles and extend you arm's reach for any rearranging that is necessary on top of the roof.

ASSEMBLING THE ROOF

STEP 2

Selecting an arbitrary spot along the wall, take your first pair and place the ends you have nailed together in the center of the yurt. These joined ends will either rest on the platform you have constructed or balanced on the tip of the pole that a friend is holding steady in the middle of the floor.

The Horizontal Piece According to the way I have instructed you to assemble the pair, the ends of each piece should be positioned as follows: your top piece, the horizontal one with the nail partially driven, should rest on top of the cable, the nail resting above the cable. The piece itself should be lodged against the left side of one wall juncture.

The Vertical Piece The second member of your first pair, the vertical, bottom piece, which has been predrilled the functional length distance from the joined ends, will then be spread 3 spaces so that it rests below the cable against the left side of your fourth wall juncture (see illustration). Once you have positioned your first pair, you can have two friends hold either piece in place while you proceed, or if you are slightly short-handed, the horizontal piece can be lashed to the cable.

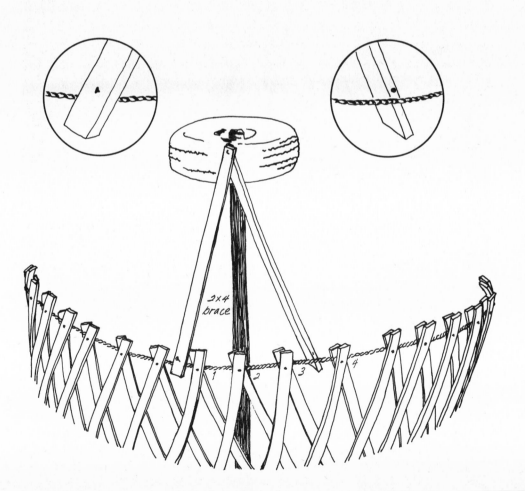

STEP 3

You are going to work counterclockwise around your wall. Therefore, take your second roof pair and move to your right 1 slot from the horizontal piece of the first pair. Position the horizontal member of your second pair in the same fashion as you did with your first horizontal piece. The joined ends will be pushed flush against your first pair, and as you shall see when you actually are doing it yourself, the second pair will sit on top of the vertical piece from your first pair. As I write this, I realize that it sounds all too confusing. My apologies for not being able to show you graphically with my own hands—but I assure you that once you begin, everything will fall into its proper place.

The vertical piece from your second pair is moved over 3 spaces so that it in fact rests at your fifth slot (see illustration). Once again, these pieces should either be held or lashed to the cable temporarily.

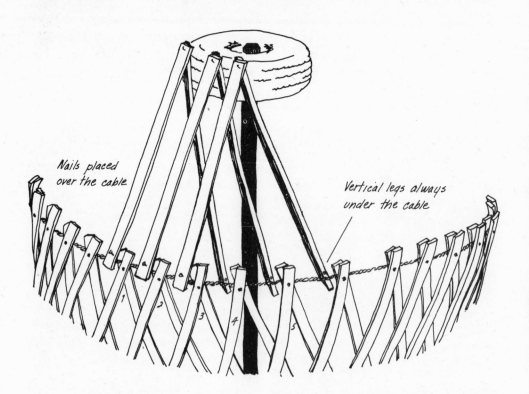

Nails placed over the cable

Vertical legs always under the cable

Next, take your third pair, move 1 slot over to your right, and place the horizontal, top piece on top of the cable, nail above the cable. The vertical, bottom member is moved over 3 spaces, as was the case with your first 2 pairs, so that is suspended below the cable at your sixth spot. Make sure that the pieces on top of the platform, or if they are being supported by poles, are knocked carefully close together. This should be done after each pair is applied to the roof.

At this time, you might want to note that you are in fact recreating the same spacing arrangement, namely a 3-foot span, that you performed with your wall.

ASSEMBLING THE ROOF

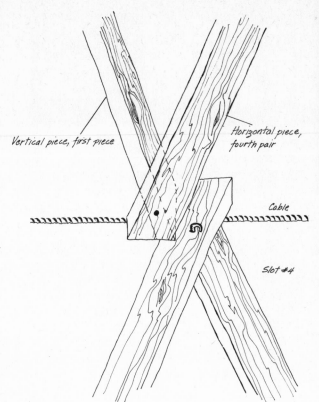

Sandwiching the cable between roof pieces; nail above the cable itself.

STEP 4

You have now come to your crucial *fourth* pair. Just as with the wall, you have a nailing surface at this time which will enable you to sandwich your cable between 2 pieces of your roof. The horizontal piece from your fourth pair rests above the cable at the fourth slot, while the vertical leg of the fourth pair is spread to the seventh slot on your wall. If you have been following instructions correctly, you will find that the horizontal leg of your fourth pair will match up with the vertical, bottom piece from your first pair. Again, it might sound confusing, but you shouldn't experience any trouble once you try it yourself. Match up the nail in the first, horizontal piece of your fourth pair with the predrilled hole in the vertical leg from the first pair. Make sure that you have the nail resting above the cable. Bracing the 2 pieces together, using your sledgehammer for a backing, the 2 pieces should be nailed together with the cable sandwiched between them. Unlike the wall, the nail should not be clenched until the entire roof is erected. The only exception to this would be if you found that the weight from the roof caused the pieces to come undone, and even here, I would recommend that you try lashing the wood together before you use clenching as a last resort. The reason I say that you should delay clenching the pairs together is that you might find weak pieces or discover that you have made some errors in positioning the wood. If this should occur, by mistake, then you would have a hard time unfastening the 1 x 2's if the nails were clenched.

To equalize weight distribution during roof assembly, you might have to switch to the opposite side of your yurt and begin roof assembly there.

STEP 5

Once you understand the principle behind the roof's construction after the fourth pair has been inserted, you should continue working counter-clockwise around the yurt, matching the horizontal and vertical pieces together correctly and nailing them in place. As you work, be sure that the skylight takes shape uniformly and that large gaps between the tops of the pairs do not develop. If you see that this is happening, your inside helpers will have to carefully nudge the pieces close to one another.

You will also want to insert more support poles, if you do not have a platform, so that no single pole is carrying a tremendous amount of weight. If you find that the yurt wall is leaning too much to one side as you add on further pairs, or if the platform starts to give way under the lopsided distribution of weight, then my recommendation to you is to lash your unattached pieces to the cable at the point you are working, and begin adding roof pieces to the opposite side, in order to equalize the weight and stress. It is not uncommon for this to occur and you should not be alarmed. When you switch to the opposite side of your wall, simply act as if you were beginning the entire procedure over again and follow steps 1 through 4. Once it appears that the wall has leveled itself out, or your platform has stabilized, you can resume on the first side where you left off before you switched. I *do not* recommend that you work in small teams in more than one area at a time, since it has been my experience that too much hammering and jockeying of 1 x 2's tends to, first of all, get confusing, and secondly, cause enough vibration to unsettle the roof and cause problems.

STEP 6

What will eventually happen as you work counterclockwise around the yurt is that you will be left with your first 3 unjoined horizontal pieces and the vertical legs from your last 3 pairs. Nail them together, maintaining the same pattern as is found in the rest of the roof. You might recognize that this is another instance where you are actually repeating the steps performed when you joined the ends of your wall together. When these last 3 matches have been made and the pieces nailed together, you should clinch all the nails against the grain of the wood.

One word of caution regarding the nailing process itself. The nail should be driven *straight* through the vertical piece. Even though you have predrilled the hole, you might find, as the roof approaches completion and its weight increases, that it will be more difficult to match the pieces so that the nail is positioned perfectly upright into the vertical, bottom 1 x 2. Do not settle for an almost perfect job—you will only end up with a not-so-perfect, not-so-strong roof later.

For a strong roof, the pieces must lie flush against one another at the skylight.

STEP 7

Check your skylight to make sure that it is perfectly round. You might find that you have to rejockey the pieces with your poles or hammer from the eaves end of the roof, until the joints line up flush in a circular design. This requires some time, but it is quite necessary if you expect to take pride in a job well done. The following pictures show what happens when this time and effort is not taken.

*Imperfect skylights are
not symmetrical and
contain unsightly gaps.*

STEP 8

Obviously, if you have not already done so, you should remove the platform or any poles that support the roof. If you have been working carefully throughout, what will occur is that your roof will naturally "sit" into position and be permanent.

STEP 9

Once you have clenched your nails at the cable, you and a friend can set about reinforcing the roof. Climb onto the roof, either from the outside of the yurt, or better still, through the skylight. Taking smaller nails (8D or 10D commons should be sufficient), you should drive nails wherever the horizontal and vertical pieces cross along the roof. Should you have a portable generator and power drill, these holes can be predrilled. If not, the nail tips should be blunted to avoid splitting.

The same thing can also be done for the wall of the yurt at the time you are reinforcing the roof. Using 8D common nails, you can very easily rigidify the wall by driving a nail through predrilled holes at points where the wall pieces intersect between the floor and the cable. These nails should be driven from the inside, so that the ends of the nails will be clenched on the outside and remain unseen when the yurt is covered.

Since you have not as yet cut yourself a door, I would suggest that you leave a 4–6-foot span of the lattice wall unreinforced. This way, there will be a section flexible enough to permit passage into and out of the yurt until you decide on how your door is to be constructed and exactly where it will be placed.

STEP 10 (Optional)

Congratulations! You have yourself a yurt skeleton, the makings of a beautiful home for you and your yaks. In several of the yurt projects I have been involved with, it has been customary for the largest member of the crew to climb atop the roof, spreading his or her feet between the edges of the skylight, and pound their chest ferociously, jumping up and down occasionally, looking down upon the rest of the group. Known as the "King Kong Test," it is regarded as the symbolic gesture to the gods for a successful yurt beginning. Or if you care to be more rational and subdued, you might very well wish to express your gratitude to humans and spirits alike by having all those who have helped climb inside and sit quietly reviewing their triumph.

Completed yurt superstructure; the tire platform has not yet been removed.

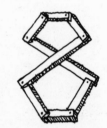

CHAPTER

*November 17 . . . the stove finally arrived three days ago from Alabama—
just in the nick of time. For a while there I thought I'd have to move into the
caboose or cabin, especially after what happened early Sunday morning. I
awoke about 2:30, after having fallen asleep reading a few hours before. The
first thing I noticed was that despite the heat from the two-burner cooking stove,
which I had continued to run in intervals since dinnertime, and the two
kerosene lamps, condensation came from my nose and mouth each time I
breathed. In addition to this indication of the temperature, I saw that Molly had
crawled to the bottom of my sleeping bag in an attempt to keep warm. Moving
around quickly to restart the circulation in my body. I stopped to readjust the
burners and read the thermometer hanging on the wall—36 degrees! My eyes fell
upon the skylight, where I noticed a constant barrage of white stuff coming
down to the forest floor. Looking from the back window, I saw that several
inches of snow had already fallen and lightly blanketed my one or two cords of
firewood, which sat there useless as could be. But this is all behind me. As I sit
here relaxed and warm, reading, writing, and dozing from time to time, the only
thoughts that are related to that cold Sunday morning are that in a few hours
I'll add a few more unsplit logs for the night's fire and open the door a crack to
let in the cool night breeze. . . .*

CUTTING DOORS
AND WINDOWS

Cutting Doors and Windows

There are very few steadfast rules regarding the addition of doors and windows. Initially, I believed that yurt dwellers in America were somewhat reluctant to remove any pieces from the skeleton, unless it was absolutely necessary. There may have been a feeling that by making the wrong cut, the entire yurt would be affected and substantially weaker. As a result, the only openings and sources of light and air were the skylight atop the roof and a small door. The plastic or plexiglass covering the roof hole would be framed and placed on a hinge, so that it could be propped open to provide a certain amount of ventilation. Unfortunately, the earlier yurts that I have seen are stuffy; even on the brightest of days, the lighting is barely adequate.

As people began to experiment with various door-and-window configurations, it became more obvious that there was little threat to the durability of the yurt if these apertures were constructed and reinforced properly. The reason for this is quite simple: because weight and tension are so evenly dispersed throughout the building by the very nature of its design, the stress placed on the individual members is minimal. Therefore, whenever minor deletions are made, the interdependence of the structure will enable surrounding pieces to assume the minor burden that was designated to the missing section of wood.

Designing and Cutting the Door

There are other people besides Omar and his friends who used to give me grief about my yurt, owing to their inability to comprehend the structure. I remember the time my father was looking over a series of pictures my sister had taken of my home while visiting me at college. As he looked them over he came to understand the yurt and appreciate it, only as a man who loved to work with wood and provide for himself can do. He stopped when he came to the one taken of my door and turned to me. "Tell me," he said, "did you intend for your door to look like a coffin, or is it mere coincidence?"

Indeed, I must admit that the shape of the door does bear a slight resemblance to a coffin. Maybe this accounts for the reluctance of so many older people in the area to step inside and take a look. In fact, come to think of it, I do recall that several of the poeple used to mispronounce my name and address me as Lon Chaney. Seriously, though, there were a number of reasons for the door being shaped the way it was. First of all, this design enabled me to leave the greatest number of pieces from the lattice wall intact. Thinking back upon it, I guess I still had my doubts about the advisability of deleting too many individual pieces at the time that I was getting around to cutting the door. At any rate, I had to make relatively few cuts and reposition a minimal number of 1 x 2's, to achieve an opening large enough to accommodate the easy passage of my body and all my material possessions, including my favorite large sugar barrel.

The second reason I selected this shape was that after close inspection, it appeared to me that since the boundaries of the door followed the natural lines of the lattice, this was in fact the least distracting and offensive opening I could make. One of the most appealing things about the yurt that I constantly mention is the sense of continuity that one feels while inside. It seems to me that every attempt should be made to ensure that as little as possible is done to desecrate this particular feature of the structure.

Once you have decided the shape you want your door opening to take, you should mark off the outline of the design on the outside of the yurt wall, so that you do not become confused later. Then make both an interior and exterior frame around the designated area, using lumber that is similar to, definitely not much heavier than, the type of wood you have utilized in the rest of the superstructure. I was originally instructed to frame the doors and windows with 2 x 4's, but I found that such material was too bulky and conspicuous in appearance. Instead, I switched back to a 1 x 2 border on the inside and outside of the wall, which provided me with a permanent, rigid frame. The gaps between interior and exterior are then filled with additional, smaller pieces of fitted 1 x 2's. This way, when it comes time to add a door jamb (inside frame), you will find that you have created an adequate nailing surface and solid area surrounding the door. In fact, once you are finished building the frame, you will see that the door and window areas are sturdier than the rest of the yurt.

As soon as you have completed the border, you can cut out and remove the correct 1 x 2 strips that are found within the frame. You might find that for the spots that are more difficult to reach, a keyhole saw or coping saw with a

The "coffin door" configuration is merely one option you might wish to consider.

heavier blade will be required. Small blocks of 1 x 2 should be placed on the floor on each side of the door opening, so that the space is perfectly stationary.

A few hints and words of caution regarding the construction of the frame for your door: One mistake that is commonly made that will lead to an eyesore is that I have observed people driving too large a spike from the outside of the wall through all 1 x 2 components of the frame, so that the nail point protrudes into the interior of the yurt. Naturally, when these nails are clenched, they are not the most attractive sight.

One other problem that develops is that people will sometimes not place their filler pieces of 1 x 2 flush with interior and exterior lattice. What occurs is that when it comes time to install the door jamb, it is difficult to have the wood sit uniformly on the solid surface you have painstakingly assembled.

My last recommendation is for you not to make the door too high. The top of the frame should be at least 6 inches below the cable. In one instance, I observed that a friend brought the door too close to the top of the wall, and this placed too much stress on the wall junctions above. What eventually had to be done was that 2 x 4 braces had to be added to prevent the cable from lagging at this particular spot. Thus, although you might have to stoop a bit more to get inside the yurt, it appears that this minor inconvenience far outweighs the consequences.

CUTTING DOORS
AND WINDOWS

Building the Actual Door

Very little has to be said about how you construct the door. As long as it shelters you from cold blasts of air, shields you from inclement weather, and prevents animals and insects from entering your home, you can go about using materials you have at your disposal. After these basic requirements are met, it's all a question of personal taste.

Personally, I preferred a heavier, more substantial door, and so I used roughcut 1 x 8 hemlock slabs. A draft-free surface was achieved by making half-lap joints between the individual pieces. For greater cross-support, I used strips of the same material.

Friends of mine wanted a lighter arrangement, and utilized ¾-and 1-inch exterior plywood. The only drawback to using plywood alone is that it has a tendency to warp if it is left uncoated. Should you select plywood, be sure to add 2 coats of linseed oil or other commercial preservative before hanging the door.

A third option, which combines a bit of the weight afforded by the solid door, but is less cumbersome, is to make a light skeleton from 1 x 2, 1 x 3, or 2 x 3 scraps and then cover both sides of this frame with ½-inch exterior plywood. The advantage of this door is that the space between the 2 layers provides an area of dead air, which acts as a natural insulator.

Whatever the material you choose, you should always use felt or rubber weather stripping on the door or along the jamb to create a more adequate seal from the wind. In addition, 1 x 1 strips should line the jamb to act as a door stop. Most likely, your door will open on an angle if it follows the natural lines of the lattice. This will place more stress on the hinges when the door is open and closed. Therefore, when you select hinges, you should look for ones that are normally used on heavier doors which are hung in the traditional manner.

Windows can be designed in many shapes and sizes.

Windows in the Yurt

At the time I was installing windows in my first yurt, time and money were my most important concerns. Rather than expending a great deal of effort searching for more attractive window designs, I settled for an old barn window donated by Omar. Although it provided me with a good source of light and ventilation, I was never completely satisfied with my decision, for it seemed to me as time wore on that the rectangular frame, with its 3 panes of glass, clashed with the assortment of diamond shapes found throughout the rest of the interior.

Looking at the pictures found below and on the preceding page, one can readily see what a difference it makes when the person takes his or her time in deciding on a more thought-out window configuration. In addition to providing a great deal of light to the yurt, these oddly shaped openings highlight the lattice design. It is far more breathtaking to wake in the early-morning hours

Yurt windows can easily be made to accent the skeletal structure.

and see the sun shimmering gloriously through these diamond portals than it is through some unexciting square or rectangular window. This is not to mention the beautiful array of distinctive shadows that find their way onto the walls and floor as a full moon sweeps across the sky.

Coming upon a yurt like this, where the builder has taken time to utilize the skeletal strips themselves in outlining the windows, the observer has a much clearer idea, without ever having entered the dwelling, of how it was erected and why it stands apart from every other type of home.

There are an infinite number of possibilities for window combinations that will maintain and accent the structural cohesiveness of the lattice frame. Tiny, individual portals can serve as peepholes in all directions, ensuring constant cross-ventilation as well. Or if you want, groups of adjacent 1 x 2's can form large openings that look out upon a particularly picturesque view. There are simply no limits as to how your windows can be assembled.

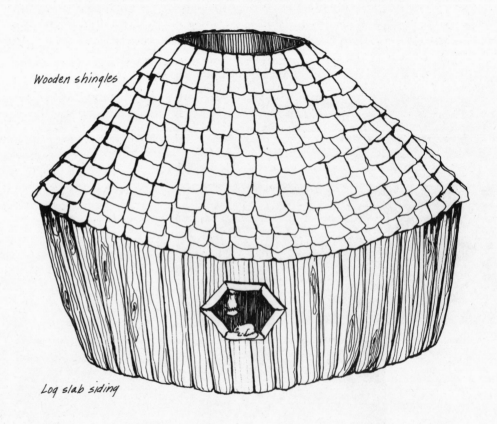

Wooden shingles

Log slab siding

Construction

Windows similar to these are relatively easy to make. Variations are quite adaptable to suit personal tastes and degrees of expertise. The first step in this operation is performed before any of the outer coverings are applied. Nail 3 or 4 layers of 1 x 2 scrap material onto the outside of the yurt wall to define your window area and give adequate support for the box casing you will insert once you have tacked on the first 4 outside layers to your yurt frame. (These are canvas or burlap, insulation, plastic vapor barrier, and felt tar paper, applied in that order.) When these materials have been wrapped around the walls and roof and are permanently fastened, you can use ¾-inch or 1-inch stock of 6–8-inch width, and construct an interior casing. This diamond-shaped chamber, with the ends of the 4 individual sides beveled to form tight-fitting joints, will be positioned inside the 1 x 2 pieces, so that the entire affair only slightly protrudes out from the yurt. Thin strips of molding material can be nailed inside the casing to form a stop for your glass, while small amounts of putty on the outside will form a water and windproof seal. If you wish to have these small portals open and close, small hinged frames can be set within the casing.

There are, of course, less complicated ways to construct windows, and they do not necessarily have to take the shape I have prescribed. A few warnings, however. Whatever the design or shape of the openings, always try to build a supportive, outward-extending 1 x 2 frame before you apply your translucent or transparent covering. Failure to do so will force you to compress insulation at these points, substantially cutting back on the thermal retention potential of your insulating material.

I do not recommend that you cut any windows in the roof. They are difficult to encase properly and I have yet to see a yurt with roof portals other than the skylight that does not leak.

CHAPTER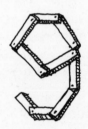

January 2 ... "Confessions of a City Slicker," or "Lost in the Yukon" I have just returned from Christmas vacation with my folks in New York. After traveling nearly six and a half hours through the blinding snow on treacherous Route 17, I finally arrived at the farmhouse. Squeezing into my already loaded rucksack a grocery bag's worth of goodies from my mother, I strapped on the snowshoes that I had been storing in my parent's house, hoisted the rucksack onto my back, grabbed my duffel bag, and began the ½-mile trek to the woods.

It is still coming down like crazy as I sit here writing, and I must report that I had a hell of a time finding the doorway to the woods. The visibility was next to nothing and there were no tracks to guide me, since the trail has not been been used these two weeks that everyone has been away. I must have walked back and forth along the forest perimeter and backtracked the field, attempting to correct my miscalculations a dozen times, before I found the inconspicuous tunnel opening to the woods. Once I reached the yurt, I realized that in my haste to get going the day I left, I'd forgotten to put aside kindling and a few dry logs for the first fire. I searched around and came up with some dead twigs hanging on the trees around the yurt. I hope it won't be long before the wood dries out and catches in the stove, relieving the residue of numbness I still feel in my right

COVERING THE YURT *toe. ... I can hardly wait until Omar spots my tortuous tracks in the snow*

Covering the Yurt

tomorrow morning. Maybe I can sneak out early enough to avoid his wisecracks about my meandering pilgrimage.

Of all the occupations I have undertaken during my rather short lifetime, there is none that has been as worthwhile as building my own home. The simple chores, duties, and routines that took up most of my time during this period left me knowing myself—feeling better about my performance as a human being than anything I had previously done. Even the most menial of repetitive tasks that were involved never reverted to tedium, since I was totally cognizant of the significance of my efforts. My days flew by incredibly fast, and at the end of each one I felt physically exhausted, yet mentally more alert and refreshed than when I had begun. For I could stand back from the yurt and actually *see* what I had accomplished.

Once the initial frame was raised, I worked alone most of the time. When I received assistance, it was not that such aid was truly necessary. I think back on it and see that people were helping for their own benefit as well as for mine. Again, it was quite simply a case of people taking advantage of the rare opportunity we all have these days, to be neighborly, and it has made the entire project that much more memorable for me.

Concealing the Insulation—Layer 1

Unless you've grown a tremendous attachment to the sight of aluminum foil, you will want to cover the frame of the yurt with some layer of material to screen off the shiny facing of the fiberglass insulation. There are a number of opaque fabrics I mentioned earlier (see page 33) that will serve this purpose, and I will now review and elaborate on them further.

The first lining you could use is a combination of old quilts and blankets. Colorful and light though they might be, most of the time the patterns divert from the natural beauty of the lattice, and therefore rarely would I ever select this option.

Secondly, you can utilize burlap feed bags. They are relatively inexpensive, quite novel, and easy to apply. There are, however, two drawbacks you should be aware of before you go out and make your purchase of a hundred or so of these bags. They are extremely flammable and I would strongly urge you to soak each one sufficiently in a commercial fireproofing solution before you tack them on the wall. My second observation is that they tend to darken with

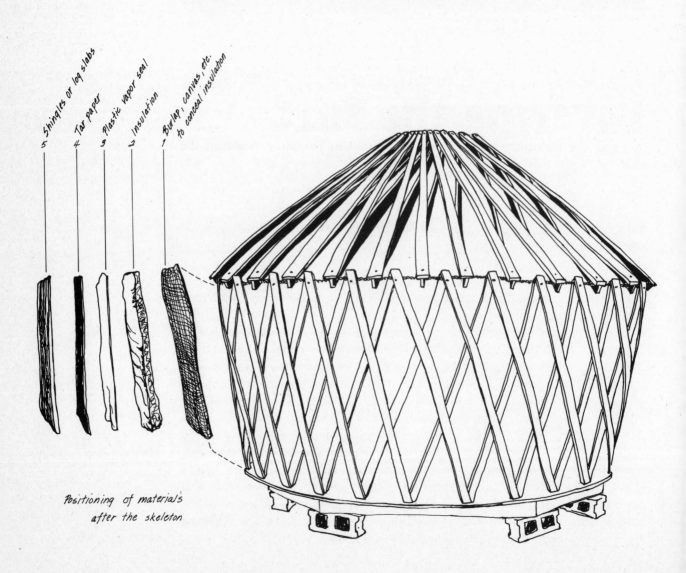

Shingles or log slabs 5
Tar paper 4
Plastic vapor seal 3
Insulation 2
Burlap, canvas, etc. to conceal insulation 1

Positioning of materials after the skeleton

Author's yurt: the first winter.

age and might very well end up creating an interior environment that is darker than you originally planned. For this reason, you might want to saturate them with a mild bleaching solution to lighten the burlap. One other mistake I made the time I used burlap was that I split the bags along the seam to cover the maximum surface area per unit. Unfortunately, however, the resulting screen was not opaque enough to completely mask the aluminum side of the insulation. Although it might cost you a few dollars more, you end up with a more appealing covering when the bags are left whole.

A third type of material for concealing the insulation, which I have observed being used in yurts quite successfully, is white canvas. Although your initial outlay of money might be greater for canvas, it is the easiest to work with and creates a magnificent effect—I say this because of the way it subtly highlights the intricate design of the lattice skeleton.

There are, of course, other materials that I have not mentioned, which can be employed to serve the same purpose. Some you might wish to think about are a plain muslin fabric, simple bamboo curtain material, or perhaps even army-surplus parachutes if they are handy.

Applying the Cover

The way the material is applied is just as important as the type of covering itself. If you don't work conscientiously or display craftsmanship, anything you use will destroy the interior appearance of your home. Using a heavy-duty stapling gun, loaded with 5/16-inch staples, has been found to be the easiest, neatest means to fasten your fabric to the outside of your wall. The material should be drawn tightly enough that there are no wrinkles. If you are using individual sheets or burlap bags, they should be attached singly, leaving a sufficient overlap. This is particularly true for your roof. When you come to an opening in your wood—a door, window, or your skylight, I learned it was best to leave these areas for last, coming back and piecing together the material carefully at my leisure. In order to avoid a raveled and threaded border at these places, I folded the edges over an inch or so to form an even outer seam.

If you are unable to complete the entire job in a single day, be sure to cover what work you have finished with plastic. Even if it fails to rain, heavy formations of dew can permanently stain a light surface or cause it to eventually sag and look sloppy.

Insulating the Yurt

As mentioned earlier in the book, the type of material I am most familiar with is commercially sold fiberglass insulation. In the case of my own experience, in addition to those of many friends who have built yurts, it was found that of all the products available on the market, rolls of fiberglass or mineral wool were the materials most readily obtainable. Other important reasons for its acceptance in permanent lattice-yurt construction are easily understood. It is not difficult to apply to the frame and provides a more than adequate barrier against both extreme cold and heat. In short, unless you have the time and resources to seek alternatives and experiment, here is one covering that has shown itself to work effectively and one you should very definitely consider while you are pricing and planning out your structure.

Applying Fiberglass

Fiberglass insulation is sold in rolls of varied lengths and widths. If possible, I would recommend that you purchase rolls of 24-inch width, since in the case of the 6-foot-high wall, you will encounter the least amount of difficulty in fitting the rows together and covering the entire surface. This holds true for the roof as well, where you will be positioning small pieces to form concentric circles leading up to the skylight.

There is very little that has to be said regarding attaching the insulation. Obviously it is placed over your burlap or canvas lining with the aluminum side facing the interior. For the walls, simply wrap the roll around the perimeter, beginning at the bottom and working up to the cable. Using the paper border provided for a stapling surface, fasten the material to the 1 x 2 struts with 9/16-inch staples. Once you have finished covering the entire wall, you will want to nail on the additional strips I spoke of on page 27, to serve as a hard backing for subsequent layers. Placing them at intervals of 2–3 feet, these pieces will be nailed to the edge of the floor and the eaves section of your roof struts.

Insulating the roof is a bit more tricky a process. Concentric rows of fiberglass are tacked to the roof, beginning at the base of your eaves and working toward the skylight. You will most likely discover that as you get higher along the roof, the pieces will diminish in length to accommodate the

Insulation, in this case fiberglass, is placed over the yurt superstructure.

sharper curves of your smaller circles. In yurts where pieces of insulation of uniform length were cut and applied throughout the entire roof, the end result was lumpy in appearance. Besides being unattractive, such roofs retained heat poorly and were more unmanageable when it came time to adding smooth layers of tar paper and any exterior shingling.

Whereas with your wall you waited until the entire surface was insulated before you nailed on wood strips for backing, it is best to position smaller pieces of 1 x 1's or 1 x 2's *between* each row of insulation. In this way, you are providing yourself with small "steps" for footing as you ascend the roof. Again, be careful not to utilize nails so large that they drive completely through the skeleton into the interior.

Options

Numerous experiments are being tried these days, as people seek inexpensive, effective, noncombustible insulation materials. Tests with foam sprayed onto a chicken-wire base, thin layers of polyurethane liners, forming pockets of dead-air space, mud and straw, sod—the list goes on and on. For further information regarding alternatives in insulation, you might very well want to speak to a local building contractor for advice and guidance. If you come across viable options that work successfully for you, I would be interested in hearing about them.

Adding the Vapor Barrier

The next covering to apply, once you have added your insulation, is a plastic vapor barrier. For this purpose, you should have purchased sheets of 6-mil plastic. The polyethylene is draped and wrapped around the yurt and tacked where you have placed your additional strips of wood. You will most likely find that the plastic will have to be pieced together in the roof, since it is rarely sold in sheets wide enough to cover the entire surface of the truncated cone. Leave at least 8–10 inches of overlap between each sheet and have all seams run vertically if possible. Once you have tacked the pieces on top of one another, using 9/16-inch staples, it is best to apply a thick coat of tar roofing adhesive at the seams to prevent leaks from developing. It is also wise to tar wherever you suspect water could eventually seep into the yurt—i.e., along borders of your doors, windows, or skylight. Once you have completely attached the plastic, you should check the entire operation for small holes where the staple has ripped the plastic. These spots should be plugged with tar.

Hint: For easy application of tar take one of your discarded roof pieces and wrap an old towel around one end. This "tar brush" will enable you to reach all seams on your roof without difficulty.

Moving Right Along . . .

A mistake that is sometimes made, once the vapor seal has been added, is that people think they can lie back and relax, for their home is now guarded against moisture. A lazy fellow, whom I liken to the grasshopper in the famous ant-grasshopper fable, thought just this. Unfortunately, a severe storm decided to drop in and say hello, bringing with her a housewarming gift of torrential rains and 40–50 mile-an-hour winds. By the time she left, the plastic had ripped free from the frame, and all around his yurt clumps of fiberglass rested idly on the ground, insulating an anthill, providing stuffing for the field mouse's winter home. I wish I had taken a picture. The area looked like the cotton candy stand at the county fair.

Tar Paper

A medium-weight felt tar paper will add more water and wind protection to the outside of the yurt. It is not a costly item and is relatively simple to apply.

For the wall, start at the bottom on one side of your door and wrap your roll of tar paper around the entire yurt, stapling as you go along. It is important that you begin at the bottom and that subsequent rows positioned above are overlapped 3 or 4 inches onto the layer below. This is done so that water running down the wall will not meander underneath and cause an unexpected leak. Before you position each additional row of paper onto the one below it, it is best to add a thin coat of tarring on the upper border of the bottom sheet. When you overlap the paper onto this sticky surface, the resulting seam will be more permanent. It will also make it easier for the over coat of tar to adhere without annoying breaks and bubbles in the seam. When you come to within a few inches of the top of the wall, it is best to chisel out with a utility knife and fit your final layer of tar paper so that it squeezes neatly between your roof struts. Naturally there will be a larger overlap for your final row of tar paper.

Once you have finished the wall, you may want to apply small dabs of tar over your staples to ensure a waterproof surface. This operation can be done with either a putty knife or thin scrap of wood.

One suggestion regarding windows in the wall: because it is likely that they will be oddly shaped, you might find it most efficient to first cover them over with tar paper and later cut them out from the inside. Doing it this way and adding small bits of tar and paper where it is required, there will be less opportunity for leaks to spring up due to awkward seams and patching.

When it comes time to tar paper the roof, you should perch yourself through the skylight, standing on either a ladder or a makeshift sawhorse scaffolding. Starting at your skylight, leaving a substantial lip which can be removed later, staple one end of a precut length of paper to the edge of your circular opening, and unroll the paper toward the bottom of the roof. When determining the length of your individual strips, you should take into account the fact that they will be positioned diagonally toward the eaves of the roof, rather than being suspended straight to the bottom. The reason for this arrangement soon becomes apparent. Otherwise, it would be difficult to maintain substantial overlaps for the many sheets of paper, and more footage of materials would actually be required.

Once you have fixed that paper at the proper angle (25–30 degrees), you should reach down and staple it to the small auxiliary strips of wood. Wherever you cannot reach from the skylight will have to be tacked from a stepladder, lest you find that a permanent seal is harder to achieve later on.

The operation might differ, according to the size of your skylight and the angle at which you drop the paper down the roof. You may discover that somewhere during the papering process you have to decrease the angle or even crisscross a piece or two against the arrangement of all the other strips of felt in order to completely cover the roof. In any event, make sure that you maintain a wrinkle-free surface. Between each strip, adequate overlapping should be made and each seam should be treated with tar adhesive in the same fashion as was done for the wall. When you have finished covering the roof, add small dabs of tar where you have stapled and neatly remove the superfluous flaps of paper around your skylight and at the eaves, to form continuous circular patterns.

Finishing the Yurt

I have involved myself on several occasions in arguments regarding the yurt and the question of aesthetic appearance versus function. Indeed one can discuss differing points of view concerning the portable design as opposed to the permanent lattice yurt, as opposed to the solid-board configuration. In this area, I can see conversations as being worthwhile and informative for the participants. But something that seems to be beyond the realm of debate is the matter of a messy, thrown-together yurt, with a patchy, wrinkled tar-paper exterior left as the final outer layer. Why in the world do we need another kind of eyesore in the countryside?

For most people who opt for a yurt as their shelter, hopefully the major factors involved in their decision go beyond its cost and the relative ease with which one is assembled. If those were the main concerns, it stands to reason they would simply put together a ramshackle cabin composed of scraps and donations, or buy a prefab plywood shanty. Allow me to have another crack at what yurts are all about, as seen through the eyes of many a yurt builder. Yurts represent a visible effort that some people are displaying to move forward and radically redirect the course of their lives, using their own minds and bodies to alter the semblance of their environment. Once the break seemingly has been made with the traditional, self-perpetuating mediocrity of modern society, inroads toward actual change and improvement are more easily grasped by the individual. Yurts have helped some people realize their own potential to be part of social as well as individual progress, and if a person's potential is merely the chaotic ugliness of tar paper and blotches of exposed fiberglass, then that's too bad. Perhaps they should be off to "Walden Breezes" Trailer Park, where they are now showing the latest in Swiss Chalet Mobile Homes.

One rationale offered to me after I commented upon the outward appearance of an unfinished yurt was that the person who had built it could not afford to shell out more money to complete it. In this case, this simply was not true. With a sizable sawmill operation nearby and the owner perfectly willing to donate log slabs to anyone who had the means to haul them away from his mill, it appeared that it would have been quite easy to finish the yurt. It was just absurd that he could have worked so diligently on the frame and application of outer layers, only to leave it incomplete with just one more layer to go.

Working with Log Slabs

The first cuts of a tree on a large sawmill yield slabs that in most cases are useless in the mill operation. In the yurt structure, however, they create an attractive rustic exterior when applied correctly. The procedure is not difficult, though it is a timely process and requires patience, if the job is to be done right. Since you will be positioning the slabs vertically around the yurt, it will be necessary to place horizontal strips over the tar paper to serve as a backing for your siding. These extra pieces will run perpendicular to the vertical struts

Yurt with log slabs.

used as backing for your plastic and tar paper, and in fact will be nailed to them directly. Once this has been done, the slabs can be pieced together to form an even surface, free from unattractive bulges from large knots and other irregularities in the wood. This matching takes some time but is well worth the bother. If you prefer a more-finished look, the bark can be removed and one of the many outdoor wood stains applied once the slab has been smoothed sufficiently.

There are other ways to finish the yurt than log slabs and I will mention a few others I have observed or heard about. If you have the time and money, you can employ wood shingles. I have also seen staggered strips of roughcut pine pieced together to form attractive siding. Other people have experimented with a stucco layer applied to a thin meshed chicken wire base. Again, it is a matter of personal taste, yet it seems there are many things that can be done to enhance the exterior of the yurt.

Finishing the Roof

The simplest, least expensive exterior surfacing for the top of your yurt is mineral roofing paper. Heavier and more durable than your felt paper, this material can be applied in very little time to make for a plain yet appealing outer layer. You might want to consider the possibility of using asbestos shingling instead. This is a bit more costly and requires more time and patience. If you want to get more sophisticated, you can use wood shingles. Here again, you will have to first nail onto your roof wooden strips for a backing before you attach these thin pieces.

Cedar shingles make
an attractive, durable
roof covering.

For a roof gutter above your doors and windows, it is easy to utilize tin cans. After you have collected as many uniform cans as are required, the bottoms are removed and all edges curled inward to prevent people from brushing against them and getting cut. The cans are fastened individually to the underside of the eaves to form a continuous runoff channel above the door or window. A thin layer of tar or other sealant is then applied to the inside of the tin can trough, while paint that blends in with the rest of the yurt can be added to the outside surface.

Covering Windows

Translucent plastic of the same weight and variety as was used for your vapor barrier can line your window openings if you cannot afford glass or pieces of plexiglass to fit these oddly shaped portals. These can be on hinged frames so that they open and close, or they can be permanently fixed to the yurt. If optical clarity is important, then you might look into one of the clear vinyl materials manufactured and sold commercially.

Finishing the Skylight

"The tent is the sky," she said, making a gesture to indicate a covering dome. "The hole in the roof is the Sun in the Sky, the Eye of Heaven, through which comes light," she continued, "and when, in the morning, we use the

"Sacred geometry!"

*chuchulir (a carved wooden dipper) to pour the tea offering on the hearth iron, the vapor goes up with the smoke to Burkhan [God]."**

One of the most striking features of the permanent lattice yurt is the design of the skylight. Viewing this center opening from below, you begin to realize the power of the circle. If there ever were such a thing as "sacred geometry," this is the pattern for which the distinction was made. With all the lines in the roof whirling to the sky and outward, the yurt is a perfectly natural structure. The "eye" of the yurt anoints the entire room with an awelike omniscience, and once the initial shock is behind you, the yurt becomes the most secure and comfortable place you can inhabit.

If at all possible, nothing should distort light from pouring through this opening. It appears to me that a transparent membrane is of the essence, if the full value of the skylight is to be appreciated. Because of its precarious position, subject to tumbling branches and the weight from a heavy snowfall, I do not recommend regular glass to be used for this purpose. Instead the shell should be composed of any of the harder, more resilient synthetic products like clear plastic or plexiglass. For further ideas on possible coverings, you can consult the *Whole Earth Catalog*, looking under the heading "Windows," Here you will find an array of suggestions and addresses concerning this subject.

In any case, the layer you apply can either remain stationary or preferably be placed on a hinged frame, which can be raised to provide

*Schuyler Cammann, *The Land of the Camel, Tents and Temples of Inner Mongolia* (New York: Ronald Press Company, 1951), p. 124. An old woman is speaking of the religious nature of her yurt.

COVERING THE YURT

117

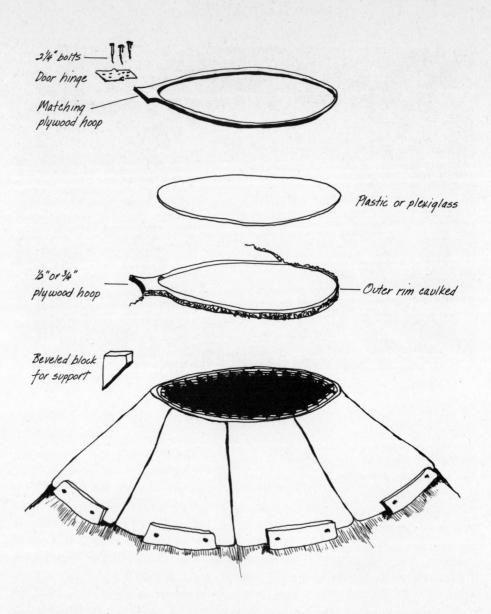

2¼" bolts

Door hinge

Matching plywood hoop

Plastic or plexiglass

½" or ¾" plywood hoop

Outer rim caulked

Beveled block for support

ventilation and serve as yet another portal for the passage of smoke and cooking fumes.

If you decide to frame your window, one easy way to do this is to use ½-inch or ¾-inch plywood. Making 2 circular hoops of identical dimensions with a small lip for your hinge, the plastic or plexiglass can be sandwiched between them. This frame should be an inch or so wider than the diameter of the opening, so that it will sit snugly over the hole. If you are using any covering that has any thickness to it, like plexiglass, the piece should be centered on one plywood hoop, with window caulking added on the outside to prevent it from sliding—also creating a more permanent seal. The other doughnutlike piece is then placed over the plastic, with small brads nailed along the perimeter to keep the 3 layers together.

When it comes time to hinge the skylight, select the largest hinge you possibly can, substituting small nuts and bolts for screws. Most likely a beveled block will have to be added to the roof outside the skylight area to

provide a regular surface for the other side of the hinge. You would also be wise to insert a layer of felt or rubber weatherstripping between the roof and the window. This gasket will prevent any moisture from seeping into the yurt. During the summertime, it is not difficult to add mosquito netting or a thin mesh screen to keep insects and animals from entering your home. Should forest critters be enough of a nuisance year-round, you might consider such a shield as a permanent addition.

If you anticipate heavy accumulations of snow, you might want to order an egg-shaped piece of plexiglass for adequate runoff. Should you be utilizing a sheet of lighter transparent plastic, two alternatives are to make a spider brace frame, consisting of smaller triangular units, similar to those used in Chuck Cox's yurts seen above, or run 3 or 4 curved strips of wood or metal withing the borders of the window. One thing I noticed about curved skylights is that they catch the rays from the sun more than a flat surface. Thus you find more light cascades through the roof, showering the interior with a greater radiance.

"You see that quarter moon up there? "Omar asked me one evening as I was preparing to leave. "See how she's tipped up there like a rockin' chair? Well that means we're in for our first heavy spring thunderstorm. Better tie down your yurt before you go to school tomorrow 'cause if you don't, she may not be there when you get back."

Betty wriggled the spot where her missing toe used to be and concurred with what her husband had already stated as fact. "From what my bones tell me, those winds could get up near fifty to sixty miles an hour. Maybe even a tornado comin! I sure hope your ert don't fly away."

I thanked them for the warning and headed home. When I woke the following morning, the sun was streaking in and nowhere in the sky was there a cloud to be seen. I flipped on the radio to hear a forecast calling for continued sunshine with a high in the low 70's. Hearing this, I dressed for a warm day and left my rain poncho hanging on the wall. When I spotted Omar sitting on the back porch, my eyes went skyward as my palms searched enlessly for the downpour. "O.K., smarty, you'll see." Pointing to the barely visible moon, Omar went on as I jumped into my car. "I sure hope you closed the windows in the yurt."

The sun continued to shine throughout the early afternoon hours. Not

The Yurt Interior

until I was on the road heading back around four o'clock did I spot a group of
ominous black clouds come rolling in from the southeast, a sure sign that
something was amiss. The wind picked up suddenly and the temperature
dropped about 15 degrees inside of five minutes.

By the time I reached the farm, hail the size of golf balls was bouncing off
the roof of my car. I parked at the edge of the woods and started to run, getting
soaked and stung with a thousand balls of hail. I was amazed when I stopped at
the cabin for a moment's relief, only to find that the building was actually
shaking from the force of the wind. If this were happening to the cabin with its
skeleton of 6 x 6 barn timbers, I didn't want to think what shape my yurt was in
by now. Despite these misapprehensions I flew from the cabin and ran for home.
When I reached the entrance I threw the door open and stepped inside, the door
resounding with a crash as the wind slammed it shut. All I could now hear were
dull thuds of hail on the roof and the muffled monsoonlike whirlwinds sweeping
around the walls. I lit a small fire to get the chill out of the room and dry my
drenched clothing, lying back on my bed to relax and catch my breath. The last
thing I recall before I dropped off was wondering whether or not Omar's
150-year old fortress of a home would survive this wicked storm.

A nice thing about designing and constructing your own home is that you piece it together slowly and are constantly remodeling the interior. There is always some improvement to make tomorrow to create a cozier and more appropriate place to live. I liken the yurt to a tight ship ready for an ocean voyage. Everything has its place and if done properly there is always room for moving about, despite the abundance of necessary supplies and equipment. I guess it never dawned on me how much room my 16-foot yurt afforded me until I decided to clean her from top to bottom on one of the first sunny spring weekends. Furniture, clothing, tools, books, cooking utensils—I removed everything I owned short of the wood stove. When I had finished clearing the yurt, I peered out the door to see a collection of stuff that could have filled a house three times its size. I couldn't believe I had accumulated all these things, and what's more, that they all fit in my tiny home. Indeed the most significant realization at this time was that I had never felt cramped or cluttered in the yurt. There was a natural order to my interior environment —things that were often needed were readily accessible, while those items that I rarely used could be neatly tucked away in their own designated place.

The availability of usable space in such a seemingly small area is visually appreciated when I tell you I once entertained nine people in my humble home. The cooking was done outside on an open fire, yet we all sat on the floor or atop my sleeping loft passing food and drink with ease. Maybe we didn't feel cramped because we were amongst friends in the most congenial of surroundings, caught up in the exuberance of such an experience. If this be the case, then so much more should be said for the yurt's inherent attraction. I would not trade an evening like that for all the spacious dining halls in the world.

A Place to Sleep

The secret behind a spacious yurt is never to clutter the center. In cases where people insisted on placing anything besides a scatter rug in the middle of the floor, the results are generally always disastrous. A mood of confinement is immediately conveyed when a person enters a yurt to discover some bulky item taking up this, the focal point of the dwelling. The symmetry of the structure is destroyed and you are unable to appreciate the functional beauty that sets the yurt apart from square or rectangular shelters. Everything you design into the interior should blend in with the geometry of the building.

I likened my home earlier to the well-laid-out ship and it seems that in many instances this is a good model to guide you when you are constructing functional furniture. For example, one type of sleeping loft that works well inside the yurt resembles the captain's bed, with its assortment of shelves and compartments. Run a piece of 2 x 4 between 9 and 12 feet in length (depending upon the width mattress you will be using) across one side of the yurt, so that you are only deleting a relatively small segment of your circular floor space. The ends of the 2 x 4 are actually fastened to your wall, resting on the spot where 2 of the 1 x 2 lattice struts intersect. You might want to add a block underneath or even a section of 2 x 4 along the wall to the floor, for further

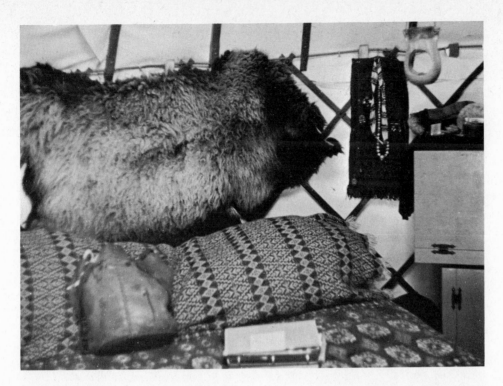

Interior of Chuck Cox's Mongolian-like yurt.

support. Then supplement 2 or 3 perpendicular slats for firm mattress support and finish the bed surface with ½-inch plywood, roughcut slabwood (sanded of course), or finished 1 x 12-inch boards. Under the bed you have your choice. You can either leave a completely unobstructed storage area or build in a series of shelves, drawers, or individual compartments, custom designed for your own needs.

A simpler arrangement, which also works well, is a hinged bed platform, which folds away during the day or seconds beautifully as a workbench when the mattress is removed.

A third bed design I have observed is a series of three rectangular storage bins, which when placed side by side form a comfortable sleeping area. Inside these boxes any number of clothes or tools can be safely stowed and are always handy.

More Furniture

In geometry, the straight line that joins the two end points of an arc of a circle is known as a *chord*. In the case of the built-in bed, this is in fact the label we give to the longer piece of 2 x 4. Chord construction can also be utilized when it comes time to put together other furniture inside. For example, a large desk or kitchen area can be designed in the same fashion. Rather than bring in some bulky chair that belongs in someone's Victorian living room, why don't you consider this: a sizable sitting area, which utilizes the naturally slanted wall for its backrest, can easily be installed by cutting a smaller arc in a quiet side of the yurt. The bench you come up with can be covered with a plush cushion, while pillows line the wall behind the seat. What greater luxury can one ask for in his or her home than a comfortable place to sit that isn't in the way?

Bookshelves can be built simply or display a more elaborate flair. The nicest thing about fastening shelves to your walls in the yurt is that your mini-beams that constitute the skeleton, are right in front of you. If you have ever stood endlessly knocking on plastered walls listening for the studs, then you know perfectly well what I'm talking about. Looking at the picture below, you get a pretty good idea of how simple it is to add neat, functional space-saving shelving. If you are interested in longer mantel-like ledges, you boards can be shaped to conform to the curve of the wall and be supported by braces at either end and in the middle.

Heating the Yurt

A salient feature of the yurt's shape that helps us understand its attraction to the Mongolian nomad is the relative ease with which the inside is kept warm during the colder months in the year. This has also been the experience for American yurt dwellers as well. Remembering the many cozy evenings I sat comfortably in my home watching the thermometer plummet way below zero, I can very well testify to the building's ability to efficiently retain heat. Only on the most brutal of winter nights was I conscious of the outside temperature as presenting any problems, and here again it was merely a question of stoking the fire, adding a few dry logs, and adjusting the flow of air into the stove.

Whatever the source of heat you select for your yurt, whether it be wood, some form of bottled gas, hard coal, even bricks of dried yak-dung, there are two basic suggestions I have to offer. First of all you needn't purchase a large stove, for you simply do not need a giant fire to keep you warm. In addition, people who have installed larger units have found it difficult to close the damper or other oxygen-varying devices down far enough so that they were still not scorching hot and uncomfortable. My second suggestion is that the fire box itself be a closed one. Fireplaces are certainly pleasing to look at but they are also terribly inefficient, as you probably already know. Besides providing little heat compared to the amount of fuel they consume, they tend to be drafty.

One type of stove becoming more and more popular among yurt dwellers is the Ashley thermostatic burning circulator, manufactured in Alabama. Once you get over the fact that in some ways it resembles an old 1920's clothes dryer and you stop looking for the place to add your nickel, you'll come to appreciate and depend on it. This unique kind of stove has a bimetal helix coil, which acts as a thermostat and regulates air intake, oftentimes without the use of any damper arrangement. Because it works on the principle of semicomplete combustion, it requires much less wood than an ordinary stove.

Three *musts* for wood stoves of any variety: First, you have to run a "thimble" between the layers of material, insulation, etc., in your wall and the stovepipe itself. Otherwise you are looking for a fire and a heap of rubble. Secondly, your stovepipe should be higher than the peak of your roof. Failure to extend the chimney this high might result in an inadequate suction of air from the fire box, and subsequently inefficient fires. Thirdly, your stove should be far enough away from the wall that the canvas or burlap fabric does not get dangerously warm while the stove is operating. Usually this means a minimum of 2-feet distance. For further safety and peace of mind, you might be wise to insert a sheet of asbestos between the stove and the wall surface.

CHAPTER 11

April 23 . . . his gray beard and deep furrows, which lined his tawny brow, would have normally led me to suspect that he was a man getting on in years. Still, one could see that he was more alert and agile than most men are in their prime. Everything that surrounded him was aware of his presence and sought his recognition and approval. I began to notice this shortly after I had picked him up walking along the road leading from town. The first indication was the unusually powerful, yet pleasing scent of the smoldering fire that greeted us as we entered the woods. Then he nodded his acknowledgment as the turgid stream, swollen from two days of constant rain, roared a welcome. Later as the flickering lamplight cast his distorted silhouette upon the lattice, he smiled and looked up as a flock of returning honkers settled on the nearby swamp. He was a most extraordinary rover—able to startle and arouse each one of my senses, as if they had been lying dormant awaiting his arrival. We filled the evening with food, wine, and soothing conversation, until neither one of us could keep the other awake. My eyes opened once during the night to see the old man stretched out on his tattered bed roll, sleeping next to the fire. I awoke to discover he had left. He had split and neatly stacked a dozen or so logs and tucked a short note between two pieces of firewood. It read:

FINAL THOUGHTS:
LOOKING AHEAD

Final Thoughts: Looking Ahead

Thanks. You have made yourself a fine place to think, drink, and ramble. I appreciate your sharing food, comforts and conversation with me for one evening. If I'm ever back this way, I'll be sure to stop by and visit again. Continue to live well and keep warm.   Eli

Hobo, poet, or prophet? A fine stranger who brought grace and humility to the yurt one rainy night in April.

A s more people in America have heard about yurts and constructed them for human inhabitance, there has been a concerted effort conducted by yurt builders of both lattice and solid-board design to determine how else such a unique structure can serve the needs of man. To give you some idea of the yurt's potential, allow me to pass on to you some of the options for the structure that come from a number of directions. There are first those things I have personally observed and participated in regarding yurt projects. Secondly, there are alternatives uses I have heard about from others. Thirdly, there are those ideas that as of the time of this writing remain personally untested, coming via conversations with many other people, on such varied subjects as architecture, ecology, and the general topic of improving the quality of education and experience in America. I provide such a section in this book in hopes that more people will attempt further experimentation and pass their discoveries to the rest of us so that we may all benefit.

A Private Place: a Web in the Circle

There are often those times when a person feels that he or she has to get away and be alone. The yurt, isolated from main dwellings, is a perfect structure for such a purpose. It is inexpensive and easy to build, adaptable enough to conform to the physical surroundings of any environment. A family-man friend of mine often complained that even in his spacious home, he still had nowhere to escape and listen to himself think. He eventually asked me to help him build a yurt, which we subsequently did. Besides constructing this special place with his own two hands, this in itself providing him with great satisfaction, he spends much of his time when daily existence starts to get him down, building a small wood fire in the yurt and afterward reading a good novel or simply napping. His wife writes me that he is much easier to live with, and come summertime, their next project is to build her one as well on the opposite end of their property.

A Place for Playing

This past summer I set out to build a ten-foot yurt on the small rural campus of a graduate school I was then attending. My original idea was to

design an insular environment for study and solitude that could be used by anyone at anytime. Unfortunately, owing to numerous distractions, I never got further than the completion of the skeleton. I left in September to begin teaching, vowing to resume the work the following spring. When I returned to visit a few months later, I found that the yurt had been taken over by some 20-odd kindergarten-age children who were attending a school that had been set up on the grounds. Here was a monkey bars the likes of which they had never seen. With two long pieces of sturdy lumber spanning the interior, they were free to roam anywhere within or on top of the yurt. Never have I observed such a fine place where children were able to use their imaginations without any boundaries or restrictions being imposed on them by any labeled item (like swings, seesaw, or slide, names that define their use immediately) designated by adults. When a teacher told them that it was called a yurt, what in fact did that mean to them in reference to any piece of playground equipment they had ever played on before? It was anything they wanted, whether that be a rocketship soaring toward Mars or a giant spider trapping them in its clutches. Other times it was dubbed the quiet room, where young minds sat conjuring up fantasies to shock their teacher or a place to complete the portrait of their latest best friend. Or perhaps they had an assignment to name all the shapes they saw within the skeleton. In other words, because it was such an amorphous design, previously unseen and so obscurely titled, it was a more valuable vehicle on which their imaginations could ride indefinitely. Anything went and all activities were acceptable. What had begun as a sanctuary for big people turned beautifully into a children's haven.

FINAL THOUGHTS:
LOOKING AHEAD

129

A Place for Stowing

Some of the ugliest things I've ever seen are the aluminum storage sheds cropping up all over, which are used to store anything from bicycles to gardening equipment. It isn't even a case of their being inexpensive, because this they certainly are not. Think of it from the point of view of the things calling this eyesore their home. I mean if you were a hoe, rake, pitchfork, lawnmower, garden hose, or bag of sheep manure, wouldn't you prefer to say that you lived in a yurt? Before you answer this question, think a minute and try to be yuman. The yurt is also an adequate structure to house an array of pets, farm animals, stores grains; maintain a workshop; or even provide an enclosed space for a small greenhouse.

A Place for Going

I have heard of a small alternative elementary school somewhere in the Maine countryside that was told that, in order to conform to local health codes, there would have to be two separate outhouses for boys and girls. The former farmhouse-turned-schoolhouse had one dilapidated privy that was quite inadequate in the eyes of the local parents and officials. To remedy this problem they constructed two sturdy five-foot yurt outhouses, covered them with thatch and log slabs, and labeled them his and hers. A finer place to contemplate and take care of business there has never been.

Yurts and Education

The teacher who winds endlessly through a maze of tedium and mediocrity can do little more than set up identical barriers for the students who follow. Since its introduction into the United States by Bill Coperthwaite more than ten years ago, the yurt structure has graphically demonstrated to people that they can take an active role in making important decisions affecting how they live. It would appear to me that education, as it has come to be defined in this country today, affords people few opportunities to effectively convey this concept to others. Speaking as someone who has utilized the yurt-building process to perform such a function, although certainly not to the extent as Coperthwaite, I have also observed that the finished yurt transcends the edifice itself. Allow me to explain. One obstacle hindering many young people from receiving fine educations in America is that they are confronted with a goal-oriented society where the end product is still something they are convinced should be worked toward and held dear. There is nothing wrong with achievement, as long as you do not forfeit the significance of the experiences involved in reaching that distinction. Too often I am afraid, however, this is exactly what occurs. The journey toward fruition takes place along the surface, and rarely is there the effort made to delve below and truly comprehend the nature of our involvement. The repeated failure to test and investigate the human potential can only lead to a vacuous existence filled

Canvas-covered Mongolian yurt found at the Meeting School in Rindge, New Hampshire.

with boredom and passivity. Doing something as simple as building a yurt can provide marvelous exposure for a young person to understand the options he or she has and prepare him to accept the challenges later to be confronted.

Obviously there are resourceful parents and educators all over who select other models than a yurt as their tools or vehicle to enlighten the young people they come in contact with, and make them more cognizant of their own abilities. It's just nice to know that here is another method that works. One last item I might mention is that once the yurt is built, it serves beautifully as a classroom to further open lines of communication between people, or as a small living arrangement at a school. What better way for several people to get to know themselves, as well as one or two roommates, in such a naturally intimate, meaningful setting?

FINAL THOUGHTS:
LOOKING AHEAD

Where Do We Go From Here?

The word "yurt" is starting to become more familiar to many Americans and other Westerners as well. From time to time I come across or am sent by friends brief articles for local papers throughout the country that deal with the subject of yurts and their American dwellers. Large city newspapers occasionally attempt to stump their readers by including the bizarre clue "a Mongol's felt tent" as part of their intricate crossword puzzles, while some people are beginning to consider yurts more and more as another option to study when designing a simple home. There is really very little doubt in my mind that yurts will increase in popularity and, in fact, why shouldn't they? They are beautiful, practical and relatively inexpensive to erect. They enable the industrious yet inexperienced lay carpenter to work with his or her own hands and build a home displaying imagination and craftsmanship.

Yet as more individuals involve themselves with yurt construction it seems it is crucial for people to further establish lines of communication and share with others their own triumphs and experiments in yurt design. Hopefully the yurt idea will not be exploited, coopted, corrupted or diluted beyond the point of recognition, as has so often been the case with other alternative ideas in living and education. To sum it all up I can only say that yurts are for humans who choose to live simply and take pride and learn from experiences which lead them into areas previously unknown. May I wish you luck, happiness and much success in your yurty adventure.

More on Yurts and Yurt Construction

For additional plans and information write:

1. Chuck Cox plans for the original Mongolian lattice yurt.
   Chuck Cox
   c/o The Meeting School
   Rindge, New Hampshire
2. Bill Coperthwaite for information and plans regarding solid board yurt construction and yurt workshops.
   William Coperthwaite
   Bucks Harbor, Maine 04618

For further information on the original yurt and their nomadic inhabitants consult the following books and magazine articles:

1. C. R. Bawden, *The Modern History of Mongolia* (London: Frederick A. Praeger Publishers, 1968).
2. Schuyler Cammann, *The Land of the Camel, Tents and Temples of Inner Mongolia* (New York: The Ronald Press Company, 1951).
3. *National Geographic Magazine;*
   a) January 1936, "With the Nomads of Central Asia," by Edward Murray
   b) March 1962, "Journey to Outer Mongolia," by William O. Douglas

c) April 1972, "Winter Caravan to the Roof of the World," by Sabrina and
Roland Michaud

4. Herbert Harold Vreeland, III, *Mongol Community and Kinship Structure,*
Human Resources Area Files (HRAF) Press, New Haven, Connecticut, 1962

Miscellaneous

1. Foam Insulation. Write:
Lloyd Fox
Douglas and Sturgess
730 Bryant Street
San Francisco, California 94107

Materials Supply Company
Box 28307
Sacramento, California 95828

Dow Chemical Company
Construction Materials
Midland, Michigan 48640

2. Ashley Thermostatic Wood Burning Circulator. Write:
Ashely Automatic Heater Company
P.O. Box 730
Sheffield, Alabama 35660

FINAL THOUGHTS:
LOOKING AHEAD

Index